SAN FRANCISCO RESTAURANT GUIDE 2014

RESTAURANTS, BARS & CAFES

☆☆☆☆☆

The Most Positively Reviewed and Recommended Restaurants in the City

EGP Editorial

SAN FRANCISCO RESTAURANT GUIDE 2014
Recommended Restaurants, Bars & Cafés

© Allen A. Ginsberg, 2014
© E.G.P. Editorial, 2014

Web: http://www.EGPGuides.com/

Printed in USA.

ISBN-13: 978-1501075629
ISBN-10: 1501075624

Copyright © 2014
All rights reserved.

SAN FRANCISCO RESTAURANT GUIDE 2014
Most Recommended Restaurants in San Francisco

*This directory is dedicated to San Francisco Business Owners and Managers
who provide the experience that the locals and tourists enjoy.
Thanks you very much for all that you do and thank for being the "People Choice".*

*Thanks to everyone that posts their reviews online and
the amazing reviews sites that make our life easier.*

*The places listed in this book are the most positively reviewed
and recommended by locals and travelers from around the world.*

*Thank you for your time and enjoy the directory that is
designed with locals and tourist in mind!*

TOP 500
RESTAURANTS
Ranked from #1 to #500

#1
Crepe-Madame Catering
Cuisines: Crêpes
Average price: Under $10
Area: Dogpatch, Potrero Hill
Address: Potrero Hill
San Francisco, CA 94107
Phone: (415) 513-9252

#2
Gary Danko
Cuisines: American
Average price: Above $61
Area: Fisherman's Wharf, Russian Hill
Address: 800 N Point St
San Francisco, CA 94109
Phone: (415) 749-2060

#3
Lou's Cafe
Cuisines: Coffee & Tea, Sandwiches
Average price: Under $10
Area: Inner Richmond
Address: 5017 Geary Blvd
San Francisco, CA 94118
Phone: (415) 379-4429

#4
Roxie Food Center
Cuisines: Grocery, Sandwiches
Average price: Under $10
Area: Mission Terrace, Outer Mission
Address: 1901 San Jose Ave
San Francisco, CA 94112
Phone: (415) 587-2345

#5
Old Skool Cafe
Cuisines: Soul Food, American
Average price: $11-30
Area: Bayview-Hunters Point
Address: 1429 Mendell St
San Francisco, CA 94124
Phone: (415) 822-8531

#6
M & L Market
Cuisines: Sandwiches
Average price: Under $10
Area: Castro
Address: 691 14th St
San Francisco, CA 94114
Phone: (415) 431-7044

#7
Arizmendi Bakery
Cuisines: Bakery, Pizza
Average price: Under $10
Area: Inner Sunset
Address: 1331 9th Ave
San Francisco, CA 94122
Phone: (415) 566-3117

#8
Ike's Place
Cuisines: Sandwiches
Average price: $11-30
Area: Castro
Address: 3489 16th St
San Francisco, CA 94114
Phone: (415) 553-6888

#9
The Boy's Deli
Cuisines: Deli, Sandwiches
Average price: Under $10
Area: Russian Hill
Address: 2222 Polk St
San Francisco, CA 94109
Phone: (415) 776-3099

#10
Kokkari Estiatorio
Cuisines: Greek, Mediterranean
Average price: $31-60
Area: Financial District
Address: 200 Jackson St
San Francisco, CA 94111
Phone: (415) 981-0983

#11
Deli Board
Cuisines: Deli, Sandwiches
Average price: $11-30
Area: SoMa
Address: 1058 Folsom St
San Francisco, CA 94103
Phone: (415) 552-7687

#12
Cowgirl Creamery
Cuisines: Cheese Shop, Deli
Average price: $11-30
Area: Embarcadero, SoMa, South Beach
Address: 1 Ferry Bldg
San Francisco, CA 94111
Phone: (415) 362-9350

#13
Ty Sandwich
Cuisines: Vietnamese, Sandwiches
Average price: Under $10
Area: Excelsior
Address: 4829 Mission St
San Francisco, CA 94112
Phone: (415) 333-7242

#14
Petite Deli
Cuisines: Deli, Sandwiches
Average price: Under $10
Area: North Beach
Address: 752 Columbus Ave
San Francisco, CA 94133
Phone: (415) 398-1682

#15
The Codmother Fish and Chips
Cuisines: British, Fish & Chips, Seafood
Average price: Under $10
Area: Fisherman's Wharf, North Beach/Telegraph Hill
Address: 2824 Jones St
San Francisco, CA 94133
Phone: (415) 606-9349

#16
Submarine Center
Cuisines: Sandwiches
Average price: Under $10
Area: West Portal
Address: 820 Ulloa St
San Francisco, CA 94127
Phone: (415) 564-1455

#17
V-105
Cuisines: Cafe
Average price: $11-30
Area: SoMa
Address: 105 Valencia St
San Francisco, CA 94103
Phone: (415) 525-3799

#18
Molinari Delicatessen
Cuisines: Sandwiches, Deli
Average price: Under $10
Area: North Beach/Telegraph Hill
Address: 373 Columbus Ave
San Francisco, CA 94133
Phone: (415) 421-2337

#19
L'ardoise Bistro
Cuisines: French
Average price: $31-60
Area: Duboce Triangle
Address: 151 Noe St
San Francisco, CA 94114
Phone: (415) 437-2600

#20
Good Luck Cafe and Deli
Cuisines: Deli, Cafe, Sandwiches
Average price: Under $10
Area: Chinatown
Address: 621 Kearny St
San Francisco, CA 94108
Phone: (415) 781-2328

#21
Beanstalk Cafe
Cuisines: Coffee & Tea, Sandwiches
Average price: Under $10
Area: Nob Hill, Union Square
Address: 724 Bush St
San Francisco, CA 94108
Phone: (415) 576-1966

#22
Thorough Bread & Pastry
Cuisines: Bakery, Sandwiches
Average price: Under $10
Area: Castro
Address: 248 Church St
San Francisco, CA 94114
Phone: (415) 558-0690

#23
Cheese Boutique
Cuisines: Cheese Shop, Sandwiches
Average price: $11-30
Area: Glen Park
Address: 660 Chenery St
San Francisco, CA 94131
Phone: (415) 333-3390

#24
Carmel Pizza Company
Cuisines: Pizza, Italian
Average price: $11-30
Area: Fisherman's Wharf, North Beach/Telegraph Hill
Address: 2826 Jones St
San Francisco, CA 94133
Phone: (415) 676-1185

#25
La Folie
Cuisines: French
Average price: Above $61
Area: Russian Hill
Address: 2316 Polk St
San Francisco, CA 94109
Phone: (415) 776-5577

#26
Rosamunde Sausage Grill
Cuisines: German
Average price: Under $10
Area: Lower Haight
Address: 545 Haight St
San Francisco, CA 94117
Phone: (415) 437-6851

#27
Saigon Sandwich
Cuisines: Vietnamese, Sandwiches
Average price: Under $10
Area: Tenderloin
Address: 560 Larkin St
San Francisco, CA 94102
Phone: (415) 474-5698

#28
Acquerello
Cuisines: Italian
Average price: Above $61
Area: Nob Hill
Address: 1722 Sacramento St
San Francisco, CA 94109
Phone: (415) 567-5432

#29
Crepes A Go Go
Cuisines: Crêpes, Food Stand
Average price: Under $10
Area: SoMa
Address: 350 11th St
San Francisco, CA 94103
Phone: (415) 503-1294

#30
Anchor Oyster Bar
Cuisines: Seafood
Average price: $31-60
Area: Castro
Address: 579 Castro St
San Francisco, CA 94114
Phone: (415) 431-3990

#31
Roli Roti Gourmet Rotisserie
Cuisines: Sandwiches, Food Truck
Average price: Under $10
Area: Embarcadero, SoMa, South Beach
Address: 1 Ferry Bldg
San Francisco, CA 94105
Phone: (510) 780-0300

#32
La Palma Mexicatessen
Cuisines: Mexican
Average price: Under $10
Area: Mission
Address: 2884 24th St
San Francisco, CA 94110
Phone: (415) 647-1500

#33
The House
Cuisines: Asian Fusion
Average price: $31-60
Area: North Beach/Telegraph Hill
Address: 1230 Grant Ave
San Francisco, CA 94133
Phone: (415) 986-8612

#34
Ted's Market and Delicatessen
Cuisines: Deli, Sandwiches
Average price: Under $10
Area: SoMa
Address: 1530 Howard St
San Francisco, CA 94103
Phone: (415) 552-0309

#35
Cafe Du Soleil
Cuisines: French, Coffee & Tea
Average price: $11-30
Area: SoMa
Address: 345 3rd St
San Francisco, CA 94107
Phone: (415) 699-6154

#36
Cafe Me
Cuisines: Coffee & Tea, Sandwiches, Breakfast & Brunch
Average price: Under $10
Area: Financial District
Address: 500 Washington St
San Francisco, CA 94111
Phone: (415) 288-8628

#37
La Boulange de Pine
Cuisines: Bakery, Sandwiches
Average price: Under $10
Area: Lower Pacific Heights
Address: 2325 Pine St
San Francisco, CA 94115
Phone: (415) 440-0356

#38
Chapeau!
Cuisines: French
Average price: $31-60
Area: Inner Richmond
Address: 126 Clement St
San Francisco, CA 94118
Phone: (415) 750-9787

#39
The Sandwich Place
Cuisines: Sandwiches
Average price: Under $10
Area: Mission
Address: 2029 Mission St
San Francisco, CA 94110
Phone: (415) 431-3811

#40
Frances
Cuisines: American, Salad
Average price: $31-60
Area: Castro
Address: 3870 17th St
San Francisco, CA 94114
Phone: (415) 621-3870

#41
Little Star Pizza
Cuisines: Pizza
Average price: $11-30
Area: Alamo Square, NoPa
Address: 846 Divisadero St
San Francisco, CA 94117
Phone: (415) 441-1118

#42
Frascati
Cuisines: American
Average price: $31-60
Area: Russian Hill
Address: 1901 Hyde St
San Francisco, CA 94109
Phone: (415) 928-1406

#43
Lovejoy's Tea Room
Cuisines: British, Tea Room
Average price: $11-30
Area: Noe Valley
Address: 1351 Church St
San Francisco, CA 94114
Phone: (415) 648-5895

#44
Stones Throw
Cuisines: American
Average price: $31-60
Area: Russian Hill
Address: 1896 Hyde St
San Francisco, CA 94109
Phone: (415) 796-2901

#45
Fresh Brew Coffee
Cuisines: Sandwiches, Vietnamese
Average price: Under $10
Area: Nob Hill, Union Square
Address: 882 Bush St
San Francisco, CA 94108
Phone: (415) 567-0915

#46
Hog Island Oyster Co
Cuisines: Seafood, Seafood Market
Average price: $11-30
Area: Embarcadero, SoMa
Address: 1 Ferry Bldg
San Francisco, CA 94111
Phone: (415) 391-7117

#47
Bistro Central Parc
Cuisines: French, Breakfast & Brunch
Average price: $31-60
Area: NoPa
Address: 560 Central Ave
San Francisco, CA 94117
Phone: (415) 931-7272

#48
Handy Delicatessen
Cuisines: Deli
Average price: Under $10
Area: Outer Sunset
Address: 1815 Irving St
San Francisco, CA 94122
Phone: (415) 681-3323

#49
Don Pisto's
Cuisines: Mexican
Average price: $11-30
Area: North Beach/Telegraph Hill
Address: 510 Union St
San Francisco, CA 94133
Phone: (415) 395-0939

#50
Leopold's
Cuisines: Austrian, Bar
Average price: $11-30
Area: Russian Hill
Address: 2400 Polk St
San Francisco, CA 94109
Phone: (415) 474-2000

#51
Taqueria Guadalajara
Cuisines: Mexican
Average price: Under $10
Area: Excelsior
Address: 4798 Mission St
San Francisco, CA 94112
Phone: (415) 469-5480

#52
Saison
Cuisines: American
Average price: Above $61
Area: SoMa, South Beach
Address: 178 Townsend St
San Francisco, CA 94107
Phone: (415) 828-7990

#53
La Ciccia
Cuisines: Italian, Seafood
Average price: $31-60
Area: Noe Valley
Address: 291 30th St
San Francisco, CA 94131
Phone: (415) 550-8114

#54
Sotto Mare
Cuisines: Seafood, Italian
Average price: $11-30
Area: North Beach/Telegraph Hill
Address: 552 Green St
San Francisco, CA 94133
Phone: (415) 398-3181

#55
Kawika's Ocean Beach Deli
Cuisines: Deli, Sandwiches
Average price: Under $10
Area: Outer Richmond
Address: 734 La Playa Street
San Francisco, CA 94121
Phone: (415) 221-2031

#56
Nosh This
Cuisines: Desserts, Food Stand
Average price: $11-30
Area: Dogpatch, Potrero Hill
Address: 2325 3rd St
San Francisco, CA 94107
Phone: (415) 570-9701

#57
Guerra Quality Meats
Cuisines: Meat Shop, Sandwiches
Average price: Under $10
Area: Parkide
Address: 490 Taraval St
San Francisco, CA 94116
Phone: (415) 564-0585

#58
El Farolito
Cuisines: Mexican
Average price: Under $10
Area: Mission
Address: 2779 Mission St
San Francisco, CA 94110
Phone: (415) 824-7877

#59
Central Coffee Tea & Spice
Cuisines: Breakfast & Brunch
Average price: Under $10
Area: NoPa
Address: 1696 Hayes St
San Francisco, CA 94117
Phone: (415) 922-2008

#60
HRD Coffee Shop
Cuisines: Asian Fusion
Average price: Under $10
Area: SoMa
Address: 521A 3rd Street
San Francisco, CA 94107
Phone: (415) 543-2355

#61
Garaje
Cuisines: Mexican, Burgers
Average price: $11-30
Area: SoMa
Address: 475 3rd St
San Francisco, CA 94107
Phone: (415) 644-0838

#62
Lucca Delicatessen
Cuisines: Deli, Cheese Shop
Average price: Under $10
Area: Marina/Cow Hollow
Address: 2120 Chestnut St
San Francisco, CA 94123
Phone: (415) 921-7873

#63
Tanguito
Cuisines: Argentine, Burgers
Average price: Under $10
Area: Fisherman's Wharf, North Beach/Telegraph Hill
Address: 2850 Jones St
San Francisco, CA 94133
Phone: (415) 577-4223

#64
Chez Maman
Cuisines: French, Burgers, Crêpes
Average price: $11-30
Area: Potrero Hill
Address: 1453 18th St
San Francisco, CA 94107
Phone: (415) 824-7166

#65
The Salad Place
Cuisines: American, Sandwiches, Salad
Average price: Under $10
Area: Excelsior
Address: 400 London St
San Francisco, CA 94112
Phone: (415) 333-4030

#66
Lavash
Cuisines: Persian/Iranian
Average price: $11-30
Area: Inner Sunset
Address: 511 Irving St
San Francisco, CA 94122
Phone: (415) 664-5555

#67
Golden Boy Pizza
Cuisines: Pizza, Italian
Average price: Under $10
Area: North Beach/Telegraph Hill
Address: 542 Green St
San Francisco, CA 94133
Phone: (415) 982-9738

#68
Hot Sauce and Panko
Cuisines: Chicken Wings
Average price: Under $10
Area: Inner Richmond
Address: 1545 Clement St
San Francisco, CA 94118
Phone: (415) 387-1908

#69
Swan Oyster Depot
Cuisines: Seafood
Average price: $11-30
Area: Nob Hill
Address: 1517 Polk St
San Francisco, CA 94109
Phone: (415) 673-1101

#70
Saru Sushi Bar
Cuisines: Sushi Bar, Japanese
Average price: $31-60
Area: Noe Valley
Address: 3856 24th St
San Francisco, CA 94114
Phone: (415) 400-4510

#71
State Bird Provisions
Cuisines: Tapas, American
Average price: $31-60
Area: Western Addition
Address: 1529 Fillmore St
San Francisco, CA 94115
Phone: (415) 795-1272

#72
Samiramis Imports
Cuisines: Middle Eastern
Average price: Under $10
Area: Mission
Address: 2990 Mission St
San Francisco, CA 94110
Phone: (415) 824-6555

#73
Long Bridge Pizza Co
Cuisines: Pizza
Average price: $11-30
Area: Dogpatch, Potrero Hill
Address: 2347 3rd St
San Francisco, CA 94103
Phone: (415) 829-8999

#74
Tonys Pizza Napoletana
Cuisines: Pizza, Italian
Average price: $11-30
Area: North Beach/Telegraph Hill
Address: 1570 Stockton St
San Francisco, CA 94133
Phone: (415) 835-9888

#75
Avedano's Holly Park Market
Cuisines: Meat Shop, Sandwiches
Average price: $31-60
Area: Bernal Heights
Address: 235 Cortland Ave
San Francisco, CA 94110
Phone: (415) 285-6328

#76
Thai Idea Vegetarian
Cuisines: Vegan, Thai, Vegetarian
Average price: $11-30
Area: Tenderloin
Address: 710 Polk St
San Francisco, CA 94109
Phone: (415) 440-8344

#77
House of Prime Rib
Cuisines: Steakhouse
Average price: $31-60
Area: Nob Hill
Address: 1906 Van Ness Ave
San Francisco, CA 94109
Phone: (415) 885-4605

#78
Pizzetta 211
Cuisines: Pizza
Average price: $11-30
Area: Outer Richmond
Address: 211 23rd Ave
San Francisco, CA 94121
Phone: (415) 379-9880

#79
Allegro Romano
Cuisines: Italian, Seafood
Average price: $31-60
Area: Russian Hill
Address: 1701 Jones St
San Francisco, CA 94109
Phone: (415) 928-4002

#80
Benu
Cuisines: American, Asian Fusion
Average price: Above $61
Area: Financial District, SoMa
Address: 22 Hawthorne St
San Francisco, CA 94105
Phone: (415) 685-4860

#81
Pläj Scandinavian Restaurant & Bar
Cuisines: Scandinavian, Bar
Average price: $31-60
Area: Hayes Valley
Address: 333 Fulton St
San Francisco, CA 94102
Phone: (415) 294-8925

#82
BaoNecci Restaurant
Cuisines: Pizza, Italian
Average price: $11-30
Area: North Beach/Telegraph Hill
Address: 516 Green St
San Francisco, CA 94133
Phone: (415) 989-1806

#83
Flour & Co
Cuisines: Bakery, American
Average price: Under $10
Area: Nob Hill
Address: 1030 Hyde St
San Francisco, CA 94109
Phone: (415) 992-7620

#84
Cafe Europa
Cuisines: German, Polish
Average price: $11-30
Area: Inner Richmond
Address: 4318 California St
San Francisco, CA 94118
Phone: (415) 386-1000

#85
Brenda's French Soul Food
Cuisines: Cajun/Creole, French
Average price: $11-30
Area: Tenderloin
Address: 652 Polk St
San Francisco, CA 94102
Phone: (415) 345-8100

#86
Hollywood Cafe
Cuisines: Breakfast & Brunch, Cafe
Average price: $11-30
Area: Fisherman's Wharf, North Beach/Telegraph Hill
Address: 530 N Point St
San Francisco, CA 94133
Phone: (415) 563-3779

#87
The Richmond
Cuisines: Wine Bar, American
Average price: $31-60
Area: Inner Richmond
Address: 615 Balboa St
San Francisco, CA 94118
Phone: (415) 379-8988

#88
Batter Up
Cuisines: American, Desserts
Average price: Under $10
Area: Mission Terrace, Outer Mission
Address: 888 Geneva Ave
San Francisco, CA 94112
Phone: (415) 205-6032

#89
Atelier Crenn
Cuisines: French
Average price: Above $61
Area: Marina/Cow Hollow
Address: 3127 Fillmore St
San Francisco, CA 94123
Phone: (415) 440-0460

#90
Aziza
Cuisines: Moroccan
Average price: $31-60
Area: Outer Richmond
Address: 5800 Geary Blvd
San Francisco, CA 94121
Phone: (415) 752-2222

#91
Seakor Polish Delicatessen and Sausage Factory
Cuisines: Grocery, Ethnic Food, Deli
Average price: Under $10
Area: Outer Richmond
Address: 5957 Geary Blvd
San Francisco, CA 94121
Phone: (415) 387-8660

#92
The Chairman Truck
Cuisines: Chinese, Food Truck
Average price: Under $10
Area: Tenderloin, Union Square
Address: 177 Eddy St
San Francisco, CA 94102
Phone: (415) 813-8800

#93
Caffe Ambrosia
Cuisines: Ice Cream, American
Average price: Under $10
Area: Financial District
Address: 14 Trinity Pl
San Francisco, CA 94104
Phone: (415) 362-0538

#94
Giordano Bros
Cuisines: Sandwiches, Burgers
Average price: Under $10
Area: North Beach
Address: 303 Columbus Ave
San Francisco, CA 94133
Phone: (415) 397-2767

#95
Noeteca
Cuisines: Coffee & Tea, American
Average price: $11-30
Area: Bernal Heights, Mission
Address: 1551 Dolores St
San Francisco, CA 94110
Phone: (415) 824-5524

#96
Rhea's Deli & Market
Cuisines: Deli, Sandwiches
Average price: Under $10
Area: Mission
Address: 800 Valencia St
San Francisco, CA 94110
Phone: (415) 282-5255

#97
Hot Spud
Cuisines: Gluten-Free, Fast Food
Average price: Under $10
Area: Fisherman's Wharf, North Beach/Telegraph Hill
Address: 2640 Mason St
San Francisco, CA 94133
Phone: (415) 399-1065

#98
Seven Hills
Cuisines: Italian
Average price: $31-60
Area: Nob Hill
Address: 1550 Hyde St
San Francisco, CA 94109
Phone: (415) 775-1550

#99
Monterey Deli
Cuisines: Coffee & Tea, Sandwiches
Average price: Under $10
Area: Sunnyside, Outer Mission
Address: 499 Monterey Blvd
San Francisco, CA 94127
Phone: (415) 337-8447

#100
Elephant Sushi
Cuisines: Sushi Bar
Average price: $11-30
Area: Russian Hill
Address: 1916 Hyde St
San Francisco, CA 94109
Phone: (415) 440-1905

#101
Prather Ranch Meat Company
Cuisines: Meat Shop, American
Average price: $11-30
Area: Embarcadero
Address: 1 Ferry Building
San Francisco, CA 94109
Phone: (415) 391-0420

#102
Belly Good Cafe & Crepes
Cuisines: Ice Cream, Crêpes
Average price: Under $10
Area: Japantown, Lower Pacific Heights
Address: 1737 Post St
San Francisco, CA 94115
Phone: (415) 346-8383

#103
Albona Ristorante Istriano
Cuisines: Italian
Average price: $31-60
Area: North Beach/Telegraph Hill
Address: 545 Francisco St
San Francisco, CA 94133
Phone: (415) 441-1040

#104
Sushi Zone
Cuisines: Sushi Bar, Japanese
Average price: $11-30
Area: Mission
Address: 1815 Market St
San Francisco, CA 94103
Phone: (415) 621-1114

#105
Marina Deli
Cuisines: Deli
Average price: Under $10
Area: Marina/Cow Hollow
Address: 2299 Chestnut St
San Francisco, CA 94123
Phone: (415) 346-7800

#106
First Korean Market
Cuisines: Korean, Ethnic Food
Average price: Under $10
Area: Inner Richmond
Address: 4625 Geary Blvd
San Francisco, CA 94118
Phone: (415) 221-2565

#107
Pearl's Deluxe Burgers
Cuisines: Burgers
Average price: $11-30
Area: Tenderloin
Address: 708 Post St
San Francisco, CA 94109
Phone: (415) 409-6120

#108
Griddle Fresh
Cuisines: Breakfast & Brunch, Salad
Average price: $11-30
Area: Noe Valley
Address: 4007 24th St
San Francisco, CA 94114
Phone: (415) 647-7037

#109
Jane on Fillmore
Cuisines: Coffee & Tea, Bakery
Average price: $11-30
Area: Pacific Heights
Address: 2123 Fillmore St
San Francisco, CA 94115
Phone: (415) 931-5263

#110
Harris' Restaurant
Cuisines: Steakhouse
Average price: Above $61
Area: Nob Hill
Address: 2100 Van Ness Ave
San Francisco, CA 94109
Phone: (415) 673-1888

#111
NOPA
Cuisines: American, European
Average price: $31-60
Area: Alamo Square
Address: 560 Divisadero St
San Francisco, CA 94117
Phone: (415) 864-8643

#112
4505 Meats
Cuisines: American, Butcher
Average price: $11-30
Area: Embarcadero, SoMa, South Beach
Address: 1 Ferry Building
San Francisco, CA 94111
Phone: (415) 255-3094

#113
Taqueria Vallarta
Cuisines: Mexican
Average price: Under $10
Area: Mission
Address: 3033 24th St
San Francisco, CA 94110
Phone: (415) 826-8116

#114
La Fusión
Cuisines: Latin American
Average price: $11-30
Area: Financial District
Address: 475 Pine St
San Francisco, CA 94104
Phone: (415) 781-0894

#115
Poc-Chuc
Cuisines: Latin American, Mexican
Average price: $11-30
Area: Mission
Address: 2886 16th St
San Francisco, CA 94103
Phone: (415) 558-1583

#116
Tommaso's Ristorante Italiano
Cuisines: Italian, Pizza
Average price: $11-30
Area: Financial District
Address: 1042 Kearny St
San Francisco, CA 94133
Phone: (415) 398-9696

#117
Kappa Japanese Restaurant
Cuisines: Japanese, Bar
Average price: Above $61
Area: Japantown, Lower Pacific Heights
Address: 1700 Post St
San Francisco, CA 94115
Phone: (415) 673-6004

#118
Fat Angel
Cuisines: Gastropub, American
Average price: $11-30
Area: Western Addition
Address: 1740 O'Farrell St
San Francisco, CA 94115
Phone: (415) 525-3013

#119
Kiss Seafood
Cuisines: Japanese, Sushi Bar, Seafood
Average price: Above $61
Area: Japantown, Lower Pacific Heights
Address: 1700 Laguna St
San Francisco, CA 94115
Phone: (415) 474-2866

#120
Primavera
Cuisines: Mexican
Average price: $11-30
Area: Embarcadero, SoMa
Address: 1 Ferry Plz
San Francisco, CA 94111
Phone: (415) 693-0996

#121
Cafe St. Jorge
Cuisines: Breakfast & Brunch
Average price: Under $10
Area: Bernal Heights, Mission
Address: 3438 Mission St
San Francisco, CA 94110
Phone: (415) 814-2028

#122
Cafe La Flore
Cuisines: Coffee & Tea, Sandwiches
Average price: Under $10
Area: Inner Sunset
Address: 1340 Irving St
San Francisco, CA 94122
Phone: (415) 504-6798

#123
Alimento
Cuisines: Coffee & Tea, Sandwiches
Average price: Under $10
Area: North Beach
Address: 507 Columbus Ave
San Francisco, CA 94133
Phone: (415) 296-9463

#124
Mama's on Washington Square
Cuisines: Breakfast & Brunch
Average price: $11-30
Area: North Beach/Telegraph Hill
Address: 1701 Stockton St
San Francisco, CA 94133
Phone: (415) 362-6421

#125
Cafe GoLo
Cuisines: Bakery, Breakfast & Brunch
Average price: Under $10
Area: Marina/Cow Hollow
Address: 1602 Lombard St
San Francisco, CA 94123
Phone: (415) 673-4656

#126
Firefly
Cuisines: American, Vegetarian
Average price: $31-60
Area: Noe Valley
Address: 4288 24th St
San Francisco, CA 94114
Phone: (415) 821-7652

#127
Cafe Algiers
Cuisines: Coffee & Tea, Sandwiches
Average price: Under $10
Area: Financial District, SoMa
Address: 50 Beale St
San Francisco, CA 94105
Phone: (415) 512-8681

#128
Lolinda
Cuisines: Steakhouse, Argentine, Tapas
Average price: $31-60
Area: Mission
Address: 2518 Mission St
San Francisco, CA 94110
Phone: (415) 550-6970

#129
Bar Crudo
Cuisines: Seafood, Live/Raw Food
Average price: $31-60
Area: NoPa
Address: 655 Divisadero St
San Francisco, CA 94117
Phone: (415) 409-0679

#130
Azucar Lounge
Cuisines: Mexican, Breakfast & Brunch
Average price: $11-30
Area: SoMa
Address: 299 9th St
San Francisco, CA 94103
Phone: (415) 255-2982

#131
Koo
Cuisines: Japanese, Sushi Bar
Average price: $31-60
Area: Inner Sunset
Address: 408 Irving St
San Francisco, CA 94122
Phone: (415) 731-7077

#132
Cafe La Flore
Cuisines: Coffee & Tea, Sandwiches
Average price: Under $10
Area: Inner Richmond
Address: 1032 Clement St
San Francisco, CA 94118
Phone: (415) 386-2814

#133
Underdog
Cuisines: Hot Dogs, Vegetarian
Average price: Under $10
Area: Inner Sunset
Address: 1634 Irving St
San Francisco, CA 94122
Phone: (415) 665-8881

#134
Coffee Bar
Cuisines: Coffee & Tea, Sandwiches
Average price: Under $10
Area: Mission
Address: 1890 Bryant St
San Francisco, CA 94110
Phone: (415) 551-8100

#135
Jackson Place Cafe
Cuisines: Coffee & Tea, Sandwiches
Average price: Under $10
Area: Financial District
Address: 633 Battery St
San Francisco, CA 94111
Phone: (415) 225-4891

#136
Keiko à Nob Hill
Cuisines: French, American
Average price: Above $61
Area: Nob Hill
Address: 1250 Jones St
San Francisco, CA 94109
Phone: (415) 829-7141

#137
Blue Bottle Coffee Co
Cuisines: Coffee & Tea, Cafe
Average price: $11-30
Area: SoMa
Address: 66 Mint St
San Francisco, CA 94103
Phone: (510) 653-3394

#138
Zazie
Cuisines: Breakfast & Brunch, French
Average price: $11-30
Area: Cole Valley
Address: 941 Cole St
San Francisco, CA 94117
Phone: (415) 564-5332

#139
Dinosaurs
Cuisines: Vietnamese, Sandwiches
Average price: Under $10
Area: Castro
Address: 2275 Market St
San Francisco, CA 94114
Phone: (415) 503-1421

#140
Suppenküche
Cuisines: German
Average price: $11-30
Area: Hayes Valley
Address: 525 Laguna St
San Francisco, CA 94102
Phone: (415) 252-9289

#141
Darwin Cafe
Cuisines: Cafe, Sandwiches, Salad
Average price: $11-30
Area: SoMa
Address: 212 Ritch St
San Francisco, CA 94107
Phone: (415) 800-8668

#142
Genki Crepes
Cuisines: Desserts, Crêpes
Average price: Under $10
Area: Inner Richmond
Address: 330 Clement St
San Francisco, CA 94118
Phone: (415) 379-6414

#143
Helmand Palace
Cuisines: Afghan
Average price: $11-30
Area: Russian Hill
Address: 2424 Van Ness Ave
San Francisco, CA 94109
Phone: (415) 345-0072

#144
De Afghanan Kabob House
Cuisines: Afghan, Middle Eastern
Average price: $11-30
Area: Tenderloin
Address: 1035 Geary St
San Francisco, CA 94109
Phone: (415) 929-1124

#145
La Taqueria
Cuisines: Mexican
Average price: Under $10
Area: Mission
Address: 2889 Mission St
San Francisco, CA 94110
Phone: (415) 285-7117

#146
Espetus Churrascaria
Cuisines: Steakhouse, Brazilian, Buffet
Average price: $31-60
Area: Hayes Valley
Address: 1686 Market St
San Francisco, CA 94102
Phone: (415) 552-8792

#147
Plow
Cuisines: Breakfast & Brunch, American
Average price: $11-30
Area: Potrero Hill
Address: 1299 18th St
San Francisco, CA 94107
Phone: (415) 821-7569

#148
Bite
Cuisines: Deli, Sandwiches
Average price: Under $10
Area: Tenderloin
Address: 912 Sutter St
San Francisco, CA 94104
Phone: (415) 563-2483

#149
Baker & Banker
Cuisines: American, Bakery
Average price: $31-60
Area: Lower Pacific Heights
Address: 1701 Octavia St
San Francisco, CA 94109
Phone: (415) 351-2500

#150
Arizmendi Bakery
Cuisines: Bakery, Pizza
Average price: Under $10
Area: Mission
Address: 1268 Valencia St
San Francisco, CA 94110
Phone: (415) 826-9218

#151
Zushi Puzzle
Cuisines: Sushi Bar, Japanese
Average price: $31-60
Area: Marina/Cow Hollow
Address: 1910 Lombard St
San Francisco, CA 94123
Phone: (415) 931-9319

#152
Paulie's Pickling
Cuisines: Deli, Sandwiches
Average price: Under $10
Area: Bernal Heights
Address: 331 Cortland Ave
San Francisco, CA 94110
Phone: (415) 285-0800

#153
Loló
Cuisines: Tapas
Average price: $11-30
Area: Mission
Address: 974 Valencia St
San Francisco, CA 94110
Phone: (415) 643-5656

#154
Little Star Pizza
Cuisines: Pizza
Average price: $11-30
Area: Mission
Address: 400 Valencia St
San Francisco, CA 94103
Phone: (415) 551-7827

#155
The Sandwich Spot
Cuisines: Sandwiches, Salad
Average price: Under $10
Area: Marina/Cow Hollow
Address: 3213 Pierce St
San Francisco, CA 94123
Phone: (415) 829-2587

#156
Pasta Gina
Cuisines: Deli, Sandwiches
Average price: $11-30
Area: Noe Valley
Address: 741 Diamond St
San Francisco, CA 94114
Phone: (415) 282-0738

#157
Mission Groceteria
Cuisines: Grocery, Deli
Average price: $11-30
Area: Mission
Address: 2950 23rd St
San Francisco, CA 94110
Phone: (415) 648-0275

#158
Mission Picnic
Cuisines: Sandwiches, Caterer
Average price: Under $10
Area: Mission
Address: 3275 22nd St
San Francisco, CA 94110
Phone: (415) 735-3080

#159
Burma Superstar
Cuisines: Burmese
Average price: $11-30
Area: Inner Richmond
Address: 309 Clement St
San Francisco, CA 94118
Phone: (415) 387-2147

#160
Dottie's True Blue Cafe
Cuisines: American, Breakfast & Brunch, Cafe, Coffee & Tea
Average price: $11-30
Area: SoMa
Address: 28 6th St
San Francisco, CA 94103
Phone: (415) 885-2767

#161
Marcella's Lasagneria & Cucina
Cuisines: Cafe, Italian
Average price: $11-30
Area: Dogpatch, Potrero Hill
Address: 1099 Tennessee St
San Francisco, CA 94107
Phone: (415) 920-2225

#162
Gamine
Cuisines: French, Burgers
Average price: $11-30
Area: Marina/Cow Hollow
Address: 2223 Union St
San Francisco, CA 94123
Phone: (415) 771-7771

#163
Saha
Cuisines: Gluten-Free, Arabian
Average price: $31-60
Area: Tenderloin
Address: 1075 Sutter St
San Francisco, CA 94109
Phone: (415) 345-9547

#164
Spruce
Cuisines: American
Average price: Above $61
Area: Presidio Heights
Address: 3640 Sacramento St
San Francisco, CA 94118
Phone: (415) 931-5100

#165
Amelie
Cuisines: French
Average price: $11-30
Area: Nob Hill
Address: 1754 Polk St
San Francisco, CA 94109
Phone: (415) 292-6916

#166
Crossroads Cafe
Cuisines: Coffee & Tea, Sandwiches
Average price: Under $10
Area: SoMa, South Beach
Address: 699 Delancey St
San Francisco, CA 94107
Phone: (415) 512-5111

#167
Higher Grounds Coffee House
Cuisines: Crêpes, Breakfast & Brunch
Average price: $11-30
Area: Glen Park
Address: 691 Chenery St
San Francisco, CA 94131
Phone: (415) 587-2933

#168
Enjoy Vegetarian Restaurant
Cuisines: Vegetarian, Chinese
Average price: $11-30
Area: Inner Sunset
Address: 754 Kirkham St
San Francisco, CA 94122
Phone: (415) 682-0826

#169
Isa
Cuisines: French, Gluten-Free
Average price: $31-60
Area: Marina/Cow Hollow
Address: 3324 Steiner St
San Francisco, CA 94123
Phone: (415) 567-9588

#170
Red Door Cafe
Cuisines: Breakfast & Brunch
Average price: $11-30
Area: Lower Pacific Heights
Address: 1608 Bush St
San Francisco, CA 94108
Phone: (415) 441-1564

#171
Lite Bite
Cuisines: American
Average price: $11-30
Area: Marina/Cow Hollow
Address: 1796 Union St
San Francisco, CA 94123
Phone: (415) 931-5483

#172
The Sentinel
Cuisines: Sandwiches
Average price: Under $10
Area: Financial District, SoMa
Address: 37 New Montgomery St
San Francisco, CA 94105
Phone: (415) 284-9960

#173
AK Subs
Cuisines: Sandwiches, Salad, Burgers
Average price: Under $10
Area: SoMa
Address: 397 8th St
San Francisco, CA 94103
Phone: (415) 241-9600

#174
El Castillito
Cuisines: Mexican
Average price: Under $10
Area: Duboce Triangle
Address: 136 Church St
San Francisco, CA 94114
Phone: (415) 621-3428

#175
Wooly Pig Cafe
Cuisines: Sandwiches, Coffee & Tea
Average price: Under $10
Area: Inner Sunset
Address: 205 Hugo St
San Francisco, CA 94122
Phone: (415) 592-8015

#176
Good Mong Kok Bakery
Cuisines: Bakery, Dim Sum, Cantonese
Average price: Under $10
Area: Chinatown
Address: 1039 Stockton St
San Francisco, CA 94108
Phone: (415) 397-2688

#177
Blue Hawaii Açaí Café
Cuisines: Juice Bar, Ice Cream
Average price: Under $10
Area: Financial District
Address: 2 Embarcadero Ctr
San Francisco, CA 94111
Phone: (415) 248-0011

#178
El Porteño Empanadas
Cuisines: Latin American, Argentine
Average price: Under $10
Area: Embarcadero, SoMa
Address: 1 Ferry Bldg
San Francisco, CA 94111
Phone: (415) 357-3621

#179
San Tung Chinese Restaurant
Cuisines: Chinese
Average price: $11-30
Area: Inner Sunset
Address: 1031 Irving St
San Francisco, CA 94122
Phone: (415) 242-0828

#180
Durty Nelly's
Cuisines: Pub, Irish
Average price: Under $10
Area: Outer Sunset
Address: 2328 Irving St
San Francisco, CA 94122
Phone: (415) 664-2555

#181
Estela's Fresh Sandwiches
Cuisines: Deli, Juice Bar, Sandwiches
Average price: Under $10
Area: Hayes Valley, Lower Haight
Address: 250 Fillmore St
San Francisco, CA 94117
Phone: (415) 553-6068

#182
Naked Lunch
Cuisines: Sandwiches
Average price: $11-30
Area: North Beach/Telegraph Hill
Address: 504 Broadway
San Francisco, CA 94133
Phone: (415) 577-4951

#183
Capannina
Cuisines: Italian
Average price: $31-60
Area: Marina/Cow Hollow
Address: 1809 Union St
San Francisco, CA 94123
Phone: (415) 409-8001

#184
Boulevard
Cuisines: French, American
Average price: Above $61
Area: Financial District
Address: 1 Mission St
San Francisco, CA 94105
Phone: (415) 543-6084

#185
La Méditerranée
Cuisines: Middle Eastern, Mediterranean, Armenian
Average price: $11-30
Area: Pacific Heights
Address: 2210 Fillmore St
San Francisco, CA 94115
Phone: (415) 921-2956

#186
Lers Ros Thai
Cuisines: Thai
Average price: $11-30
Area: Tenderloin
Address: 730 Larkin St
San Francisco, CA 94109
Phone: (415) 931-6917

#187
Jump Start Coffee & Grocery
Cuisines: Grocery, Sandwiches
Average price: Under $10
Area: Mission
Address: 1192 Guerrero St
San Francisco, CA 94110
Phone: (415) 642-7555

#188
Lucca Food Store
Cuisines: Deli, Ethnic Food
Average price: Under $10
Area: Outer Sunset
Address: 1899 Irving St
San Francisco, CA 94122
Phone: (415) 664-3870

#189
Palmyra
Cuisines: Mediterranean
Average price: Under $10
Area: Lower Haight
Address: 700 Haight St
San Francisco, CA 94117
Phone: (415) 896-4172

#190
Mission Cheese
Cuisines: Cheese Shop, Sandwiches
Average price: $11-30
Area: Mission
Address: 736 Valencia St
San Francisco, CA 94110
Phone: (415) 553-8667

#191
Box Kitchen
Cuisines: Southern, Burgers
Average price: Under $10
Area: SoMa
Address: 431 Natoma St
San Francisco, CA 94103
Phone: (415) 580-7170

#192
Chez Fayala
Cuisines: Sandwiches
Average price: Under $10
Area: Financial District
Address: 200 Pine St
San Francisco, CA 94104
Phone: (415) 773-1220

#193
Range
Cuisines: American, Cocktail Bar
Average price: $31-60
Area: Mission
Address: 842 Valencia St
San Francisco, CA 94110
Phone: (415) 282-8283

#194
Dolce Amore
Cuisines: Breakfast & Brunch
Average price: $11-30
Area: Lower Pacific Heights
Address: 1477 Van Ness Ave
San Francisco, CA 94109
Phone: (415) 674-7716

#195
BIX
Cuisines: American
Average price: $31-60
Area: Financial District
Address: 56 Gold St
San Francisco, CA 94133
Phone: (415) 433-6300

#196
Quince
Cuisines: French, Italian
Average price: Above $61
Area: Financial District
Address: 470 Pacific Ave
San Francisco, CA 94133
Phone: (415) 775-8500

#197
Paprika
Cuisines: Czech, German, Hungarian
Average price: $11-30
Area: Mission
Address: 3324 24th St
San Francisco, CA 94110
Phone: (415) 375-1477

#198
Pacific Catch
Cuisines: Seafood, Mexican
Average price: $11-30
Area: Marina/Cow Hollow
Address: 2027 Chestnut St
San Francisco, CA 94123
Phone: (415) 440-1950

#199
Boccalone
Cuisines: Meat Shop, Sandwiches
Average price: Under $10
Area: Embarcadero
Address: 1 Ferry Bldg
San Francisco, CA 94111
Phone: (415) 433-6500

#200
Bouche
Cuisines: French
Average price: $31-60
Area: Union Square
Address: 603 Bush St
San Francisco, CA 94108
Phone: (415) 956-0396

#201
Bereka Coffee
Cuisines: Coffee & Tea, Sandwiches
Average price: Under $10
Area: Marina/Cow Hollow
Address: 2320 Lombard St
San Francisco, CA 94123
Phone: (415) 440-4438

#202
El Farolito
Cuisines: Mexican
Average price: Under $10
Area: Mission
Address: 2950 24th St
San Francisco, CA 94110
Phone: (415) 641-0758

#203
Pizzeria Delfina
Cuisines: Pizza, Italian
Average price: $11-30
Area: Mission
Address: 3611 18th St
San Francisco, CA 94110
Phone: (415) 437-6800

#204
Millennium
Cuisines: Vegetarian, Vegan
Average price: $31-60
Area: Tenderloin
Address: 580 Geary St
San Francisco, CA 94102
Phone: (415) 345-3900

#205
Art's Cafe
Cuisines: Korean, American
Average price: Under $10
Area: Inner Sunset
Address: 747 Irving St
San Francisco, CA 94122
Phone: (415) 665-7440

#206
Super Duper Burgers
Cuisines: Burgers
Average price: Under $10
Area: Financial District, SoMa
Address: 783 Mission St
San Francisco, CA 94103
Phone: (415) 882-1750

#207
Hai Ky Mi Gia
Cuisines: Chinese, Vietnamese
Average price: Under $10
Area: Tenderloin
Address: 707 Ellis St
San Francisco, CA 94109
Phone: (415) 771-2577

#208
Mission Beach Cafe
Cuisines: American, Breakfast & Brunch
Average price: $11-30
Area: Mission
Address: 198 Guerrero St
San Francisco, CA 94103
Phone: (415) 861-0198

#209
Morty's Delicatessen
Cuisines: Sandwiches, Vegetarian
Average price: Under $10
Area: Civic Center
Address: 280 Golden Gate Ave
San Francisco, CA 94102
Phone: (415) 567-3354

#210
El Metate
Cuisines: Mexican
Average price: Under $10
Area: Mission
Address: 2406 Bryant St
San Francisco, CA 94110
Phone: (415) 641-7209

#211
Mango's Cafe
Cuisines: Deli, Sandwiches
Average price: Under $10
Area: Tenderloin
Address: 577 Geary St
San Francisco, CA 94102
Phone: (415) 440-2097

#212
Park Tavern
Cuisines: American, Breakfast & Brunch
Average price: $31-60
Area: North Beach/Telegraph Hill
Address: 1652 Stockton St
San Francisco, CA 94133
Phone: (415) 989-7300

#213
PizzaHacker - Vinyl Pop Up
Cuisines: Pizza, Street Vendor
Average price: $11-30
Area: Mission
Address: 3299 Mission St
San Francisco, CA 94117
Phone: (415) 621-4132

#214
Alexander's Steakhouse
Cuisines: Steakhouse
Average price: Above $61
Area: SoMa
Address: 448 Brannan St
San Francisco, CA 94107
Phone: (415) 495-1111

#215
Another Cafe
Cuisines: Coffee & Tea, Cafe
Average price: Under $10
Area: Nob Hill
Address: 1191 Pine St
San Francisco, CA 94109
Phone: (415) 857-5770

#216
Chiotras Grocery
Cuisines: Grocery, Deli
Average price: Under $10
Area: Potrero Hill
Address: 858 Rhode Island St
San Francisco, CA 94107
Phone: (415) 824-2353

#217
Cafe Jacqueline
Cuisines: French
Average price: $31-60
Area: North Beach/Telegraph Hill
Address: 1454 Grant Ave
San Francisco, CA 94133
Phone: (415) 981-5565

#218
Bella Trattoria
Cuisines: Italian
Average price: $11-30
Area: Inner Richmond
Address: 3854 Geary Blvd
San Francisco, CA 94118
Phone: (415) 221-0305

#219
Sushi Time
Cuisines: Japanese, Sushi Bar
Average price: $11-30
Area: Castro
Address: 2275 Market St
San Francisco, CA 94114
Phone: (415) 552-2280

#220
George's Zoo Liquor Deli
Cuisines: Sandwiches
Average price: Under $10
Area: Parkide
Address: 2560 Sloat Blvd
San Francisco, CA 94116
Phone: (415) 664-3215

#221
Kabuto Restaurant
Cuisines: Sushi Bar, Japanese
Average price: $31-60
Area: Inner Richmond
Address: 5121 Geary Blvd
San Francisco, CA 94118
Phone: (415) 752-5652

#222
Four Barrel Coffee
Cuisines: Coffee & Tea, Desserts
Average price: Under $10
Area: Mission
Address: 375 Valencia St
San Francisco, CA 94103
Phone: (415) 252-0800

#223
Gialina Pizzeria
Cuisines: Pizza, Italian
Average price: $11-30
Area: Glen Park
Address: 2842 Diamond St
San Francisco, CA 94131
Phone: (415) 239-8500

#224
Clancey's Market & Deli
Cuisines: Grocery, Deli
Average price: Under $10
Area: Outer Sunset
Address: 3960 Irving St
San Francisco, CA 94122
Phone: (415) 681-9569

#225
Daigo Sushi
Cuisines: Japanese, Sushi Bar
Average price: $11-30
Area: Outer Richmond
Address: 2450 Clement St
San Francisco, CA 94121
Phone: (415) 386-8008

#226
Freddie's Sandwiches
Cuisines: Sandwiches
Average price: Under $10
Area: North Beach/Telegraph Hill
Address: 300 Francisco St
San Francisco, CA 94133
Phone: (415) 433-2882

#227
Roam Artisan Burgers
Cuisines: Burgers
Average price: $11-30
Area: Marina/Cow Hollow
Address: 1785 Union St
San Francisco, CA 94123
Phone: (415) 440-7626

#228
Chomp N' Swig
Cuisines: Sandwiches, Bar
Average price: Under $10
Area: Inner Richmond
Address: 1541 Clement St
San Francisco, CA 94118
Phone: (415) 683-5946

#229
1058 Hoagie
Cuisines: Salad, Soup, Sandwiches
Average price: $11-30
Area: SoMa
Address: 180 7th St
San Francisco, CA 94103
Phone: (415) 552-8984

#230
Il Pollaio
Cuisines: Italian
Average price: $11-30
Area: North Beach
Address: 555 Columbus Ave
San Francisco, CA 94133
Phone: (415) 362-7727

#231
Marlowe
Cuisines: American, Brasserie
Average price: $11-30
Area: SoMa
Address: 330 Townsend St
San Francisco, CA 94107
Phone: (415) 974-5599

#232
Source
Cuisines: Vegan, Vegetarian, Pizza
Average price: $11-30
Area: SoMa
Address: 11 Division St
San Francisco, CA 94103
Phone: (415) 864-9000

#233
Guerrero Market & Deli
Cuisines: Grocery, Deli, Sandwiches
Average price: Under $10
Area: Mission
Address: 701 Guerrero St
San Francisco, CA 94110
Phone: (415) 647-2530

#234
Phat Philly
Cuisines: Sandwiches, Cheesesteaks, Chicken Wings
Average price: Under $10
Area: Mission
Address: 3388 24th St
San Francisco, CA 94110
Phone: (415) 550-7428

#235
Kitchen Story
Cuisines: Breakfast & Brunch, Asian Fusion, American
Average price: $11-30
Area: Castro
Address: 3499 16th St
San Francisco, CA 94114
Phone: (415) 525-4905

#236
Tortas Los Picudos
Cuisines: Mexican
Average price: Under $10
Area: Mission
Address: 2969 24th St
San Francisco, CA 94110
Phone: (415) 824-4199

#237
Front Cafe
Cuisines: Cafe
Average price: Under $10
Area: Potrero Hill
Address: 150 Mississippi St
San Francisco, CA 94107
Phone: (415) 437-6822

#238
Sophie's Crepes
Cuisines: Desserts, Crêpes
Average price: Under $10
Area: Japantown, Lower Pacific Heights
Address: 1581 Webster St
San Francisco, CA 94115
Phone: (415) 929-7732

#239
Fleur de Lys
Cuisines: French
Average price: Above $61
Area: Tenderloin
Address: 777 Sutter St
San Francisco, CA 94109
Phone: (415) 673-7779

#240
Olive
Cuisines: Lounge, Tapas
Average price: $11-30
Area: Tenderloin
Address: 743 Larkin St
San Francisco, CA 94109
Phone: (415) 776-9814

#241
Mission Public
Cuisines: Cafe, Breakfast & Brunch
Average price: Under $10
Area: Mission
Address: 233 14th St
San Francisco, CA 94103
Phone: (415) 525-4175

#242
Limón Rotisserie
Cuisines: Peruvian, Tapas
Average price: $11-30
Area: Mission
Address: 1001 S Van Ness Ave
San Francisco, CA 94110
Phone: (415) 821-2134

#243
Kare-Ken
Cuisines: Japanese
Average price: Under $10
Area: Tenderloin
Address: 552 Jones St
San Francisco, CA 94102
Phone: (415) 292-5273

#244
El Farolito
Cuisines: Mexican
Average price: Under $10
Area: Excelsior, Mission Terrace
Address: 4817 Mission St
San Francisco, CA 94112
Phone: (415) 337-5500

#245
Udupi Palace
Cuisines: Indian, Vegetarian, Vegan
Average price: $11-30
Area: Mission
Address: 1007 Valencia St
San Francisco, CA 94110
Phone: (415) 970-8000

#246
Foreign Cinema
Cuisines: Breakfast & Brunch, American
Average price: $31-60
Area: Mission
Address: 2534 Mission St
San Francisco, CA 94110
Phone: (415) 648-7600

#247
Old Jerusalem Restaurant
Cuisines: Middle Eastern, Mediterranean, Arabian
Average price: $11-30
Area: Mission
Address: 2976 Mission St
San Francisco, CA 94110
Phone: (415) 642-5958

#248
Sheboygan Bratwurst Stand
Cuisines: Hot Dogs
Average price: Under $10
Area: Potrero Hill
Address: 24 Willie Mays Plz
San Francisco, CA 94107
Phone: (888) 966-6966

#249
Henry's Hunan Restaurant
Cuisines: Chinese
Average price: $11-30
Area: North Beach/Telegraph Hill
Address: 1398 Grant Ave
San Francisco, CA 94133
Phone: (415) 765-0998

#250
Latin Grill
Cuisines: Cuban, Latin American
Average price: $11-30
Area: Fisherman's Wharf, Russian Hill
Address: 993 N Point St
San Francisco, CA 94109
Phone: (415) 345-8512

#251
Mojo Bicycle Café
Cuisines: Coffee & Tea, American
Average price: Under $10
Area: NoPa
Address: 639 Divisadero St
San Francisco, CA 94117
Phone: (415) 440-2338

#252
Bacon Bacon
Cuisines: Breakfast & Brunch, Cafe
Average price: Under $10
Area: Ashbury Heights
Address: 205 A Frederick St
San Francisco, CA 94117
Phone: (415) 571-8516

#253
Brioche Bakery & Cafe
Cuisines: Bakery, Coffee & Tea, Breakfast & Brunch
Average price: $11-30
Area: Chinatown
Address: 210 Columbus Ave
San Francisco, CA 94133
Phone: (415) 765-0412

#254
La Espiga De Oro
Cuisines: Mexican
Average price: Under $10
Area: Mission
Address: 2916 24th St
San Francisco, CA 94110
Phone: (415) 826-1363

#255
Tony Baloney's
Cuisines: Deli, Sandwiches
Average price: Under $10
Area: SoMa
Address: 1098 Howard St
San Francisco, CA 94103
Phone: (415) 863-1514

#256
A K Meats
Cuisines: Deli
Average price: Under $10
Area: Outer Richmond
Address: 2346 Clement St
San Francisco, CA 94121
Phone: (415) 933-6328

#257
Alamo Square Market & Deli
Cuisines: Grocery, Sandwiches, Deli
Average price: Under $10
Area: Alamo Square
Address: 535 Scott St
San Francisco, CA 94117
Phone: (415) 861-7120

#258
Little Heaven Deli
Cuisines: Crêpes, Gluten-Free
Average price: Under $10
Area: Mission
Address: 2348 Mission St
San Francisco, CA 94110
Phone: (415) 824-1293

#259
Thanh Long
Cuisines: Seafood, Vietnamese
Average price: $31-60
Area: Outer Sunset
Address: 4101 Judah St
San Francisco, CA 94122
Phone: (415) 665-1146

#260
Cafe Sophie
Cuisines: Cafe, Coffee & Tea
Average price: Under $10
Area: Castro
Address: 3463 16th St
San Francisco, CA 94114
Phone: (415) 529-2972

#261
Tekka Japanese Restaurant
Cuisines: Japanese, Sushi Bar
Average price: $31-60
Area: Inner Richmond
Address: 537 Balboa St
San Francisco, CA 94118
Phone: (415) 221-8455

#262
Walzwerk
Cuisines: German
Average price: $11-30
Area: Mission
Address: 381 S Van Ness Ave
San Francisco, CA 94103
Phone: (415) 551-7181

#263
Cordon Bleu Vietnamese Restaurant
Cuisines: Vietnamese
Average price: Under $10
Area: Nob Hill
Address: 1574 California St
San Francisco, CA 94109
Phone: (415) 673-5637

#264
Saint Frank Coffee
Cuisines: Coffee & Tea
Average price: $11-30
Area: Russian Hill
Address: 2340 Polk St
San Francisco, CA 94109
Phone: (415) 775-1619

#265
The Dark Horse Inn
Cuisines: American, Comfort Food
Average price: $11-30
Area: Crocker-Amazon
Address: 942 Geneva Ave
San Francisco, CA 94112
Phone: (415) 469-5508

#266
Ristorante Milano
Cuisines: Italian
Average price: $31-60
Area: Nob Hill
Address: 1448 Pacific Ave
San Francisco, CA 94109
Phone: (415) 673-2961

#267
Mr Pollo
Cuisines: American
Average price: $11-30
Area: Mission
Address: 2823 Mission St
San Francisco, CA 94110
Phone: (860) 912-9168

#268
The Cheese Steak Shop
Cuisines: Sandwiches, Cheesesteaks
Average price: Under $10
Area: Lower Pacific Heights
Address: 1716 Divisadero St
San Francisco, CA 94115
Phone: (415) 346-3712

#269
Sons & Daughters
Cuisines: American
Average price: Above $61
Area: Nob Hill, Union Square
Address: 708 Bush St
San Francisco, CA 94108
Phone: (415) 391-8311

#270
Mi Lindo Perú
Cuisines: Peruvian
Average price: $11-30
Area: Bernal Heights, Mission
Address: 3226 Mission St
San Francisco, CA 94110
Phone: (415) 642-4897

#271
Maruya
Cuisines: Japanese, Sushi Bar
Average price: Above $61
Area: Mission
Address: 2931 16th St
San Francisco, CA 94103
Phone: (415) 503-0702

#272
Oasis Grill
Cuisines: Middle Eastern, Greek, Mediterranean
Average price: Under $10
Area: Financial District
Address: 91 Drumm St
San Francisco, CA 94111
Phone: (415) 781-0313

#273
Heirloom Cafe
Cuisines: American, Cafe
Average price: $31-60
Area: Mission
Address: 2500 Folsom St
San Francisco, CA 94110
Phone: (415) 821-2500

#274
The Big 4 Restaurant
Cuisines: Lounge, American
Average price: Above $61
Area: Nob Hill
Address: 1075 California St
San Francisco, CA 94108
Phone: (415) 771-1140

#275
Hilda's Mart & Bake Shop
Cuisines: Bakery, Filipino
Average price: Under $10
Area: Excelsior
Address: 145 Persia Ave
San Francisco, CA 94112
Phone: (415) 333-3122

#276
Eiji
Cuisines: Sushi Bar, Japanese
Average price: $11-30
Area: Castro
Address: 317 Sanchez St
San Francisco, CA 94114
Phone: (415) 558-8149

#277
Velo Rouge Cafe
Cuisines: Coffee & Tea, Breakfast & Brunch, Sandwiches
Average price: Under $10
Area: Inner Richmond
Address: 798 Arguello Blvd
San Francisco, CA 94118
Phone: (415) 752-7799

#278
Hakkasan
Cuisines: Cantonese, Dim Sum
Average price: Above $61
Area: Financial District, Union Square
Address: 1 Kearny St
San Francisco, CA 94108
Phone: (415) 829-8148

#279
Balompie Cafe
Cuisines: Latin American
Average price: Under $10
Area: Mission
Address: 3349 18th St
San Francisco, CA 94110
Phone: (415) 648-9199

#280
La Santaneca
Cuisines: Latin American
Average price: Under $10
Area: Bernal Heights
Address: 3781 Mission St
San Francisco, CA 94110
Phone: (415) 648-1034

#281
15 Romolo
Cuisines: Tapas, Cocktail Bar
Average price: $11-30
Area: North Beach/Telegraph Hill
Address: 15 Romolo Pl
San Francisco, CA 94133
Phone: (415) 398-1359

#282
Okoze Sushi
Cuisines: Sushi Bar, Japanese, Tapas
Average price: $31-60
Area: Russian Hill
Address: 1207 Union St
San Francisco, CA 94109
Phone: (415) 567-3397

#283
Superstar Restaurant
Cuisines: Filipino, Chinese
Average price: Under $10
Area: Excelsior
Address: 4919 Mission St
San Francisco, CA 94112
Phone: (415) 585-4360

#284
Okina Sushi
Cuisines: Sushi Bar, Japanese
Average price: $11-30
Area: Inner Richmond
Address: 776 Arguello Blvd
San Francisco, CA 94118
Phone: (415) 387-8882

#285
Mozzeria
Cuisines: Pizza, Italian
Average price: $11-30
Area: Mission
Address: 3228 16th St
San Francisco, CA 94103
Phone: (415) 489-0963

#286
Galette 88
Cuisines: Crêpes, Cafe, French
Average price: $11-30
Area: Financial District
Address: 88 Hardie Pl
San Francisco, CA 94104
Phone: (415) 989-2222

#287
Yo Yo's
Cuisines: Japanese
Average price: Under $10
Area: Financial District
Address: 318 Pacific Ave
San Francisco, CA 94111
Phone: (415) 296-8273

#288
Truly Mediterranean
Cuisines: Mediterranean
Average price: Under $10
Area: Mission
Address: 3109 16th St
San Francisco, CA 94103
Phone: (415) 252-7482

#289
Cavalli Cafe
Cuisines: Cafe
Average price: Under $10
Area: North Beach/Telegraph Hill
Address: 1441 Stockton St
San Francisco, CA 94133
Phone: (415) 421-4219

#290
Taqueria Cancún
Cuisines: Mexican
Average price: Under $10
Area: Mission
Address: 2288 Mission St
San Francisco, CA 94110
Phone: (415) 252-9560

#291
Scoma's Restaurant
Cuisines: Seafood
Average price: $31-60
Area: Fisherman's Wharf, North Beach/Telegraph Hill
Address: Al Scoma Way
San Francisco, CA 94133
Phone: (415) 771-4383

#292
The Little Chihuahua
Cuisines: Mexican
Average price: Under $10
Area: Lower Haight
Address: 292 Divisadero St
San Francisco, CA 94117
Phone: (415) 255-8225

#293
Sunstream Coffee
Cuisines: Brazilian, Coffee & Tea
Average price: Under $10
Area: Laurel Heights
Address: 2884 Geary Blvd
San Francisco, CA 94118
Phone: (415) 567-5330

#294
Franchino
Cuisines: Italian
Average price: $11-30
Area: North Beach/Telegraph Hill
Address: 347 Columbus Ave
San Francisco, CA 94133
Phone: (415) 982-2157

#295
Cafe International
Cuisines: Coffee & Tea, Sandwiches
Average price: Under $10
Area: Lower Haight
Address: 508 Haight St
San Francisco, CA 94117
Phone: (415) 552-7390

#296
Papito
Cuisines: Mexican
Average price: $11-30
Area: Potrero Hill
Address: 317 Connecticut St
San Francisco, CA 94107
Phone: (415) 695-0147

#297
Assab Eritrean Restaurant
Cuisines: Ethiopian
Average price: $11-30
Area: Inner Richmond, Laurel Heights
Address: 2845 Geary Blvd
San Francisco, CA 94118
Phone: (415) 441-7083

#298
Limón Rotisserie
Cuisines: Peruvian
Average price: $11-30
Area: Bayview-Hunters Point
Address: 5800 3rd St
San Francisco, CA 94124
Phone: (415) 926-5665

#299
Tacos El Primo
Cuisines: Mexican, Food Truck
Average price: Under $10
Area: Bayview-Hunters Point
Address: Yosemite & Jennings
San Francisco, CA 94124
Phone: (415) 846-4975

#300
Universal Cafe
Cuisines: Breakfast & Brunch, American
Average price: $11-30
Area: Mission
Address: 2814 19th St
San Francisco, CA 94110
Phone: (415) 821-4608

#301
Tuba - Authentic Turkish
Cuisines: Mediterranean, Turkish
Average price: $11-30
Area: Mission
Address: 1007 Guerrero St
San Francisco, CA 94110
Phone: (415) 826-8822

#302
Hall Of Flame Burgers
Cuisines: Burgers
Average price: Under $10
Area: Parkmerced
Address: 73 Cambon Dr
San Francisco, CA 94132
Phone: (415) 584-4444

#303
Capo's
Cuisines: Italian, Pizza
Average price: $11-30
Area: North Beach/Telegraph Hill
Address: 641 Vallejo St
San Francisco, CA 94133
Phone: (415) 986-8998

#304
Hard Knox Cafe
Cuisines: Southern, Soul Food
Average price: $11-30
Area: Dogpatch, Potrero Hill
Address: 2526 3rd St
San Francisco, CA 94107
Phone: (415) 648-3770

#305
Hillstone
Cuisines: American, Steakhouse
Average price: $31-60
Area: Embarcadero, North Beach
Address: 1800 Montgomery St
San Francisco, CA 94111
Phone: (415) 392-9280

#306
Tofu Yu
Cuisines: Food Stand, Vegan
Average price: $11-30
Area: Stonestown
Address: 3251 20th Ave
San Francisco, CA 94132
Phone: (510) 204-9090

#307
Caffe Macaroni
Cuisines: Italian
Average price: $11-30
Area: Financial District
Address: 59 Columbus Ave
San Francisco, CA 94133
Phone: (415) 956-9737

#308
Love N Haight Deli
Cuisines: Sandwiches, Vegan, Vegetarian
Average price: Under $10
Area: Lower Haight
Address: 553 Haight St
San Francisco, CA 94117
Phone: (415) 252-8190

#309
Balompié Cafe #3
Cuisines: Latin American
Average price: Under $10
Area: Bernal Heights
Address: 3801 Mission St
San Francisco, CA 94110
Phone: (415) 647-4000

#310
Fino Restaurant
Cuisines: Italian
Average price: $11-30
Area: Tenderloin
Address: 624 Post St
San Francisco, CA 94109
Phone: (415) 928-2080

#311
Cafe Bunn Mi
Cuisines: Vietnamese
Average price: Under $10
Area: Inner Richmond
Address: 417 Clement St
San Francisco, CA 94118
Phone: (415) 668-8908

#312
E' Tutto Qua
Cuisines: Italian
Average price: $11-30
Area: Chinatown, North Beach/Telegraph Hill
Address: 270 Columbus Ave
San Francisco, CA 94133
Phone: (415) 989-1002

#313
SF Grill
Cuisines: Burgers
Average price: Under $10
Area: Alamo Square, NoPa
Address: 550 Divisadero St
San Francisco, CA 94117
Phone: (415) 235-4022

#314
Cafe Capriccio
Cuisines: Breakfast & Brunch, Cafe
Average price: Under $10
Area: North Beach/Telegraph Hill
Address: 2200 Mason St
San Francisco, CA 94133
Phone: (415) 772-0937

#315
Cinecitta Ristorante & Bar
Cuisines: Bar, Italian
Average price: $11-30
Area: North Beach/Telegraph Hill
Address: 663 Union St
San Francisco, CA 94133
Phone: (415) 291-8830

#316
Blue Plate
Cuisines: American
Average price: $31-60
Area: Bernal Heights, Mission
Address: 3218 Mission St
San Francisco, CA 94110
Phone: (415) 282-6777

#317
Sightglass Coffee
Cuisines: Coffee & Tea, Cafe
Average price: $11-30
Area: SoMa
Address: 270 7th St
San Francisco, CA 94103
Phone: (415) 861-1313

#318
Muracci's Japanese Curry & Grill
Cuisines: Japanese
Average price: Under $10
Area: Chinatown, Financial District
Address: 307 Kearny St
San Francisco, CA 94108
Phone: (415) 773-1101

#319
The Taco Shop At Underdog's
Cuisines: Sports Bar, Mexican
Average price: Under $10
Area: Outer Sunset
Address: 1824 Irving St
San Francisco, CA 94122
Phone: (415) 566-8700

#320
Forbes Island
Cuisines: American, Seafood
Average price: $31-60
Area: Fisherman's Wharf, North Beach/Telegraph Hill
Address: Pier 41
San Francisco, CA 94133
Phone: (415) 951-4900

#321
La Boulange de Polk
Cuisines: Bakery, Sandwiches
Average price: $11-30
Area: Russian Hill
Address: 2300 Polk St
San Francisco, CA 94109
Phone: (415) 345-1107

#322
Mission Pie
Cuisines: Bakery, Cafe
Average price: Under $10
Area: Mission
Address: 2901 Mission St
San Francisco, CA 94110
Phone: (415) 282-1500

#323
Calabria Bros
Cuisines: Caterer, Sandwiches, Deli
Average price: Under $10
Area: Excelsior
Address: 4763 Mission St
San Francisco, CA 94112
Phone: (415) 239-2555

#324
Tataki
Cuisines: Sushi Bar
Average price: $11-30
Area: Lower Pacific Heights
Address: 2815 California St
San Francisco, CA 94115
Phone: (415) 931-1182

#325
Absinthe Brasserie & Bar
Cuisines: French, Breakfast & Brunch
Average price: $31-60
Area: Hayes Valley
Address: 398 Hayes St
San Francisco, CA 94102
Phone: (415) 551-1590

#326
El Mansour
Cuisines: Moroccan
Average price: $31-60
Area: Outer Richmond
Address: 3119 Clement St
San Francisco, CA 94121
Phone: (415) 751-2312

#327
Nopalito
Cuisines: Mexican, Gluten-Free
Average price: $11-30
Area: Inner Sunset
Address: 1224 9th Ave
San Francisco, CA 94122
Phone: (415) 233-9966

#328
Boboquivari's
Cuisines: Steakhouse, Seafood
Average price: $31-60
Area: Marina/Cow Hollow
Address: 1450 Lombard St
San Francisco, CA 94123
Phone: (415) 441-8880

#329
Golden Coffee Shop
Cuisines: Diners, Breakfast & Brunch
Average price: Under $10
Area: Tenderloin
Address: 901 Sutter St
San Francisco, CA 94109
Phone: (415) 922-0537

#330
Beretta
Cuisines: Italian, Bar, Pizza
Average price: $11-30
Area: Mission
Address: 1199 Valencia St
San Francisco, CA 94110
Phone: (415) 695-1199

#331
Chez Papa Bistrot
Cuisines: French
Average price: $31-60
Area: Potrero Hill
Address: 1401 18th St
San Francisco, CA 94107
Phone: (415) 824-8205

#332
Pisto's
Cuisines: Mexican
Average price: $11-30
Area: North Beach/Telegraph Hill
Address: 1310 Grant St
San Francisco, CA 94133
Phone: (415) 317-4696

#333
Woodhouse Fish Co.
Cuisines: Seafood, Fish & Chips
Average price: $11-30
Area: Lower Pacific Heights
Address: 1914 Fillmore St
San Francisco, CA 94115
Phone: (415) 437-2722

#334
Mason Pacific
Cuisines: American
Average price: $31-60
Area: Nob Hill
Address: 1358 Mason St
San Francisco, CA 94133
Phone: (415) 374-7185

#335
Two Sisters Bar and Books
Cuisines: Bar, Gastropub
Average price: $11-30
Area: Hayes Valley
Address: 579 Hayes St
San Francisco, CA 94102
Phone: (415) 863-3655

#336
Parada 22
Cuisines: Latin American, Puerto Rican
Average price: $11-30
Area: The Haight
Address: 1805 Haight St
San Francisco, CA 94117
Phone: (415) 750-1111

#337
Anda Piroshki
Cuisines: Russian, Coffee & Tea
Average price: Under $10
Area: Bernal Heights
Address: 331 Cortland
San Francisco, CA 94110
Phone: (415) 821-9905

#338
Java Beach at the Zoo
Cuisines: Coffee & Tea, Sandwiches
Average price: Under $10
Area: Parkide
Address: 2650 Sloat Blvd
San Francisco, CA 94116
Phone: (415) 731-2965

#339
The Palace
Cuisines: Steakhouse
Average price: $31-60
Area: Mission
Address: 3047 Mission St
San Francisco, CA 94110
Phone: (415) 666-5218

#340
The Art Bistro
Cuisines: Coffee & Tea, Sandwiches
Average price: Under $10
Area: Outer Richmond
Address: 6900 Geary Blvd
San Francisco, CA 94121
Phone: (415) 379-7119

#341
Butter
Cuisines: American
Average price: Under $10
Area: SoMa
Address: 354 11th St
San Francisco, CA 94103
Phone: (415) 863-5964

#342
Trattoria Contadina
Cuisines: Italian
Average price: $11-30
Area: North Beach/Telegraph Hill
Address: 1800 Mason St
San Francisco, CA 94133
Phone: (415) 982-5728

#343
Samovar Tea Lounge
Cuisines: Tea Room, Vegan
Average price: $11-30
Area: Financial District, SoMa
Address: 730 Howard St
San Francisco, CA 94103
Phone: (415) 227-9400

#344
Wayo Sushi
Cuisines: Sushi Bar, Japanese
Average price: $11-30
Area: Lower Pacific Heights
Address: 1407 Van Ness Ave
San Francisco, CA 94109
Phone: (415) 474-8369

#345
La Boulange de Fillmore
Cuisines: Bakery, Coffee & Tea, Cafe
Average price: $11-30
Area: Lower Pacific Heights
Address: 2043 Fillmore St
San Francisco, CA 94115
Phone: (415) 928-1300

#346
Arinell Pizza
Cuisines: Pizza
Average price: Under $10
Area: Mission
Address: 509 Valencia St
San Francisco, CA 94110
Phone: (415) 255-1303

#347
Cu Co's Restaurant
Cuisines: Mexican, Latin American
Average price: Under $10
Area: Hayes Valley, Lower Haight
Address: 488 Haight St
San Francisco, CA 94117
Phone: (415) 863-4906

#348
Split Pea Seduction
Cuisines: Sandwiches, Soup, Salad
Average price: $11-30
Area: SoMa
Address: 138 6th St
San Francisco, CA 94103
Phone: (415) 551-2223

#349
Buena Vista Cafe
Cuisines: Cafe, Breakfast & Brunch
Average price: $11-30
Area: Fisherman's Wharf, Russian Hill
Address: 2765 Hyde St
San Francisco, CA 94109
Phone: (415) 474-5044

#350
Dinosaurs 2
Cuisines: Sandwiches, Vietnamese
Average price: Under $10
Area: Lakeside
Address: 2522 Ocean Ave
San Francisco, CA 94132
Phone: (415) 334-1421

#351
Rolling Out
Cuisines: Bakery, Cafe, Coffee & Tea
Average price: Under $10
Area: Parkide
Address: 1722 Taraval St
San Francisco, CA 94116
Phone: (415) 513-6054

#352
Cafe Claude
Cuisines: French
Average price: $31-60
Area: Financial District, Union Square
Address: 7 Claude Ln
San Francisco, CA 94108
Phone: (415) 392-3505

#353
Sweet Maple
Cuisines: American, Breakfast & Brunch
Average price: $11-30
Area: Lower Pacific Heights
Address: 2101 Sutter St
San Francisco, CA 94115
Phone: (415) 655-9169

#354
The Sandwich Shop
Cuisines: Deli, Sandwiches
Average price: Under $10
Area: Dogpatch, Potrero Hill
Address: 635 19th St
San Francisco, CA 94107
Phone: (415) 282-1754

#355
Cool Tea Bar
Cuisines: Cafe, Bubble Tea
Average price: Under $10
Area: Chinatown
Address: 728 Pacific Ave
San Francisco, CA 94133
Phone: (415) 781-8312

#356
Bursa
Cuisines: Middle Eastern, Turkish
Average price: $11-30
Area: West Portal
Address: 60 West Portal Ave
San Francisco, CA 94127
Phone: (415) 564-4006

#357
Just For You Cafe
Cuisines: American, Breakfast & Brunch
Average price: $11-30
Area: Dogpatch, Potrero Hill
Address: 732 22nd St
San Francisco, CA 94107
Phone: (415) 647-3033

#358
Trattoria Da Vittorio
Cuisines: Italian, Pizza
Average price: $11-30
Area: West Portal
Address: 150 W Portal Ave
San Francisco, CA 94127
Phone: (415) 742-0300

#359
Jardinière
Cuisines: French, American
Average price: Above $61
Area: Hayes Valley
Address: 300 Grove St
San Francisco, CA 94102
Phone: (415) 861-5555

#360
Michaelis Food Store
Cuisines: Grocery, Deli
Average price: Under $10
Area: Fisherman's Wharf, Russian Hill
Address: 901 N Point St
San Francisco, CA 94109
Phone: (415) 673-9708

#361
Thai Time Restaurant
Cuisines: Thai
Average price: Under $10
Area: Inner Richmond
Address: 315 8th Ave
San Francisco, CA 94118
Phone: (415) 831-3663

#362
La Santaneca De La Mission
Cuisines: Mexican, Salvadoran
Average price: Under $10
Area: Mission
Address: 2815 Mission St
San Francisco, CA 94110
Phone: (415) 285-2131

#363
Little Nepal
Cuisines: Himalayan/Nepalese
Average price: $11-30
Area: Bernal Heights
Address: 925 Cortland Ave
San Francisco, CA 94110
Phone: (415) 643-3881

#364
Tataki South
Cuisines: Sushi Bar, Japanese
Average price: $11-30
Area: Noe Valley
Address: 1740 Church St
San Francisco, CA 94131
Phone: (415) 282-1889

#365
Marnee Thai
Cuisines: Thai
Average price: $11-30
Area: Inner Sunset
Address: 1243 9th Ave
San Francisco, CA 94122
Phone: (415) 731-9999

#366
Oasis Cafe
Cuisines: Ethiopian
Average price: $11-30
Area: NoPa
Address: 901 Divisadero St
San Francisco, CA 94115
Phone: (415) 474-4900

#367
Sweet Woodruff
Cuisines: American, Salad, Sandwiches
Average price: $11-30
Area: Tenderloin
Address: 798 Sutter St
San Francisco, CA 94109
Phone: (415) 292-9090

#368
Wayfare Tavern
Cuisines: American
Average price: $31-60
Area: Financial District
Address: 558 Sacramento St
San Francisco, CA 94111
Phone: (415) 772-9060

#369
Cafe Du Nord - Temp.
Cuisines: Music Venues, American, Venues & Event Space
Average price: $11-30
Area: Duboce Triangle, Castro
Address: 2174 Market St
San Francisco, CA 94114
Phone: (415) 861-5016

#370
The Alembic
Cuisines: Bar, American
Average price: $11-30
Area: The Haight
Address: 1725 Haight St
San Francisco, CA 94117
Phone: (415) 666-0822

#371
Prubechu
Cuisines: Cafe, Puerto Rican
Average price: $31-60
Area: Mission
Address: 2847 Mission St
San Francisco, CA 94110
Phone: (415) 952-3654

#372
Golden Gate Meat Company
Cuisines: Meat Shop, Deli
Average price: Under $10
Area: Embarcadero, SoMa
Address: 1 Ferry Bldg
San Francisco, CA 94111
Phone: (415) 983-7800

#373
Domo
Cuisines: Sushi Bar, Japanese
Average price: $11-30
Area: Hayes Valley
Address: 511 Laguna St
San Francisco, CA 94102
Phone: (415) 861-8887

#374
Sammy's on 2nd
Cuisines: Sandwiches
Average price: Under $10
Area: Financial District, SoMa
Address: 84 2nd St
San Francisco, CA 94105
Phone: (415) 243-0311

#375
Frisco Fried
Cuisines: Soul Food
Average price: $11-30
Area: Bayview-Hunters Point
Address: 5176 3rd St
San Francisco, CA 94124
Phone: (415) 822-1517

#376
Minami Restaurant
Cuisines: Japanese, Sushi Bar
Average price: $11-30
Area: Outer Richmond
Address: 1900 Clement St
San Francisco, CA 94121
Phone: (415) 387-5913

#377
Outerlands
Cuisines: American, Breakfast & Brunch
Average price: $11-30
Area: Outer Sunset
Address: 4001 Judah St
San Francisco, CA 94122
Phone: (415) 661-6140

#378
PPQ Dungeness Island
Cuisines: Seafood, Vietnamese
Average price: $11-30
Area: Outer Richmond
Address: 2332 Clement St
San Francisco, CA 94121
Phone: (415) 386-8266

#379
Comstock Saloon
Cuisines: American
Average price: $11-30
Area: Chinatown
Address: 155 Columbus Ave
San Francisco, CA 94133
Phone: (415) 617-0071

#380
Cassava
Cuisines: American, Breakfast & Brunch
Average price: $11-30
Area: Outer Richmond
Address: 3519 Balboa St
San Francisco, CA 94121
Phone: (415) 640-8990

#381
Big Joe's
Cuisines: Breakfast & Brunch
Average price: Under $10
Area: Sunnyside, Outer Mission
Address: 717 Monterey Blvd
San Francisco, CA 94127
Phone: (415) 333-2878

#382
Bazaar Cafe
Cuisines: Coffee & Tea, American
Average price: Under $10
Area: Outer Richmond
Address: 5927 California St
San Francisco, CA 94121
Phone: (415) 831-5620

#383
Moya
Cuisines: Coffee & Tea, Ethiopian
Average price: $11-30
Area: SoMa
Address: 121 9th St
San Francisco, CA 94103
Phone: (415) 431-5544

#384
MaMa Ji's
Cuisines: Dim Sum, Szechuan
Average price: $11-30
Area: Castro
Address: 4416 18th St
San Francisco, CA 94114
Phone: (415) 626-4416

#385
Marengo on Union
Cuisines: American, Salad, Sandwiches
Average price: $11-30
Area: Marina/Cow Hollow
Address: 1980 Union St
San Francisco, CA 94123
Phone: (415) 441-2575

#386
The Sycamore
Cuisines: Gastropub
Average price: $11-30
Area: Mission
Address: 2140 Mission St
San Francisco, CA 94110
Phone: (415) 252-7704

#387
Sweet Chinito Coffee
Cuisines: Sandwiches, Ice Cream
Average price: Under $10
Area: Bernal Heights, Mission
Address: 3100 Mission St
San Francisco, CA 94110
Phone: (415) 821-3388

#388
La Trappe
Cuisines: Belgian, Gastropub
Average price: $11-30
Area: Russian Hill
Address: 800 Greenwich St
San Francisco, CA 94133
Phone: (415) 440-8727

#389
20 Spot
Cuisines: American, Wine Bar
Average price: $11-30
Area: Mission
Address: 3565 20th St
San Francisco, CA 94110
Phone: (415) 624-3140

#390
Nook
Cuisines: Wine Bar, Cafe
Average price: $11-30
Area: Nob Hill
Address: 1500 Hyde St
San Francisco, CA 94109
Phone: (415) 447-4100

#391
Jitlada Thai Cuisine
Cuisines: Thai
Average price: $11-30
Area: Japantown, Lower Pacific Heights
Address: 1826 Buchanan St
San Francisco, CA 94115
Phone: (415) 292-9027

#392
Java Beach Cafe
Cuisines: Coffee & Tea, Sandwiches
Average price: Under $10
Area: Outer Sunset
Address: 1396 La Playa St
San Francisco, CA 94122
Phone: (415) 665-5282

#393
Phillies
Cuisines: Sandwiches, Cheesesteaks
Average price: Under $10
Area: Crocker-Amazon
Address: 932 Geneva Ave
San Francisco, CA 94112
Phone: (415) 334-9606

#394
Fleur De Sel
Cuisines: Deli, French
Average price: $11-30
Area: Chinatown, Financial District
Address: 308 Kearny St
San Francisco, CA 94108
Phone: (415) 956-5005

#395
Mr. Pickles Sandwich Shop
Cuisines: Sandwiches, Salad
Average price: Under $10
Area: Mission
Address: 3380 20th St
San Francisco, CA 94110
Phone: (415) 826-0143

#396
San Jalisco
Cuisines: Mexican
Average price: $11-30
Area: Mission
Address: 901 S Van Ness Ave
San Francisco, CA 94110
Phone: (415) 648-8383

#397
Umi
Cuisines: Japanese, Sushi Bar
Average price: $11-30
Area: Potrero Hill
Address: 1328 18th St
San Francisco, CA 94107
Phone: (415) 355-1328

#398
KK Cafe
Cuisines: Coffee & Tea, Burgers
Average price: Under $10
Area: Lower Haight
Address: 252 Divisadero St
San Francisco, CA 94117
Phone: (415) 626-6188

#399
Cocotte
Cuisines: French
Average price: $31-60
Area: Nob Hill
Address: 1521 Hyde St
San Francisco, CA 94109
Phone: (415) 292-4415

#400
Antigua Coffee Shop
Cuisines: Coffee & Tea, Desserts
Average price: Under $10
Area: Parkide
Address: 1131 Taraval St
San Francisco, CA 94116
Phone: (415) 683-3259

#401
Freshroll Vietnamese Rolls & Bowls
Cuisines: Vietnamese, Sandwiches
Average price: Under $10
Area: Financial District, SoMa
Address: 157 4th St
San Francisco, CA 94103
Phone: (415) 348-1858

#402
Barbacco
Cuisines: Italian
Average price: $11-30
Area: Financial District
Address: 220 California St
San Francisco, CA 94111
Phone: (415) 955-1919

#403
Sugoi Sushi
Cuisines: Japanese
Average price: $11-30
Area: Mission
Address: 1058 Valencia St
San Francisco, CA 94110
Phone: (415) 401-8442

#404
Aslam's Rasoi
Cuisines: Indian, Pakistani
Average price: $11-30
Area: Mission
Address: 1037 Valencia St
San Francisco, CA 94110
Phone: (415) 695-0599

#405
Four Seasons Restaurant
Cuisines: Vietnamese
Average price: Under $10
Area: Tenderloin
Address: 721 Larkin St
San Francisco, CA 94109
Phone: (415) 674-4146

#406
Gitane
Cuisines: French, Spanish
Average price: $31-60
Area: Financial District, Union Square
Address: 6 Claude Ln
San Francisco, CA 94108
Phone: (415) 788-6686

#407
Taylor Street Coffee Shop
Cuisines: Breakfast & Brunch, Burgers, Sandwiches
Average price: $11-30
Area: Tenderloin
Address: 375 Taylor St
San Francisco, CA 94102
Phone: (415) 567-4031

#408
The Monk's Kettle
Cuisines: Gastropub
Average price: $11-30
Area: Mission
Address: 3141 16th St
San Francisco, CA 94103
Phone: (415) 865-9523

#409
B Star Bar
Cuisines: Asian Fusion
Average price: $11-30
Area: Inner Richmond
Address: 127 Clement St
San Francisco, CA 94118
Phone: (415) 933-9900

#410
Ristorante Parma
Cuisines: Italian
Average price: $11-30
Area: Marina/Cow Hollow
Address: 3314 Steiner St
San Francisco, CA 94123
Phone: (415) 567-0500

#411
Umami Burger
Cuisines: Burgers
Average price: $11-30
Area: Marina/Cow Hollow
Address: 2184 Union St
San Francisco, CA 94123
Phone: (415) 440-8626

#412
Hillside Supper Club
Cuisines: American, European
Average price: $11-30
Area: Bernal Heights
Address: 300 Precita Ave
San Francisco, CA 94110
Phone: (415) 285-6005

#413
Zero Zero
Cuisines: Pizza, Italian, Lounge
Average price: $11-30
Area: SoMa
Address: 826 Folsom St
San Francisco, CA 94107
Phone: (415) 348-8800

#414
Fable
Cuisines: American
Average price: $31-60
Area: Castro
Address: 558 Castro St
San Francisco, CA 94114
Phone: (415) 590-2404

#415
Gallardos Mexican Restaurant
Cuisines: Mexican, Breakfast & Brunch
Average price: Under $10
Area: Mission
Address: 3248 18th St
San Francisco, CA 94110
Phone: (415) 436-9387

#416
Canela
Cuisines: Spanish, Tapas Bar
Average price: $11-30
Area: Duboce Triangle, Castro
Address: 2272 Market St
San Francisco, CA 94114
Phone: (415) 552-3000

#417
Shabu House
Cuisines: Japanese, Hot Pot
Average price: $11-30
Area: Inner Richmond
Address: 5158 Geary Blvd
San Francisco, CA 94118
Phone: (415) 933-8600

#418
Hot Pot Garden
Cuisines: Chinese, Hot Pot
Average price: $11-30
Area: Parkide
Address: 1055 Taraval St
San Francisco, CA 94116
Phone: (415) 242-9388

#419
Lucky Dogs
Cuisines: Hot Dogs
Average price: Under $10
Area: Marina/Cow Hollow
Address: 2211 Filbert St
San Francisco, CA 94123
Phone: (415) 776-3647

#420
Pizzeria Delfina
Cuisines: Pizza, Italian
Average price: $11-30
Area: Pacific Heights
Address: 2406 California St
San Francisco, CA 94115
Phone: (415) 440-1189

#421
The Station SF
Cuisines: Breakfast & Brunch
Average price: $11-30
Area: Financial District
Address: 596 Pacific Ave
San Francisco, CA 94133
Phone: (415) 291-0690

#422
The Boardroom
Cuisines: Bar, American
Average price: Under $10
Area: North Beach/Telegraph Hill
Address: 1609 Powell St
San Francisco, CA 94133
Phone: (415) 982-8898

#423
Sushi Bistro
Cuisines: Sushi Bar, Japanese
Average price: $11-30
Area: Inner Richmond
Address: 431 Balboa St
San Francisco, CA 94118
Phone: (415) 933-7100

#424
Bean Bag Cafe
Cuisines: Burgers, Sandwiches
Average price: Under $10
Area: Alamo Square, NoPa
Address: 601 Divisadero St
San Francisco, CA 94117
Phone: (415) 563-3634

#425
The Fly Trap
Cuisines: Mediterranean, Persian/Iranian
Average price: $31-60
Area: Financial District, SoMa
Address: 606 Folsom St
San Francisco, CA 94107
Phone: (415) 243-0580

#426
Firenze by Night Ristorante
Cuisines: Italian
Average price: $11-30
Area: North Beach/Telegraph Hill
Address: 1429 Stockton St
San Francisco, CA 94133
Phone: (415) 392-8585

#427
New Eritrea Restaurant & Bar
Cuisines: Ethiopian, Vegetarian
Average price: $11-30
Area: Inner Sunset
Address: 907 Irving St
San Francisco, CA 94122
Phone: (415) 681-1288

#428
The Yellow Submarine
Cuisines: Sandwiches
Average price: Under $10
Area: Inner Sunset
Address: 503 Irving St
San Francisco, CA 94122
Phone: (415) 681-5652

#429
Garibaldi's
Cuisines: American
Average price: $31-60
Area: Presidio Heights
Address: 347 Presidio Ave
San Francisco, CA 94115
Phone: (415) 563-8841

#430
Woodhouse Fish Company
Cuisines: Seafood, Fish & Chips
Average price: $11-30
Area: Castro
Address: 2073 Market St
San Francisco, CA 94114
Phone: (415) 437-2722

#431
Olea
Cuisines: Vegetarian, American
Average price: $11-30
Area: Nob Hill
Address: 1494 California St
San Francisco, CA 94109
Phone: (415) 202-8521

#432
Lupa Trattoria
Cuisines: Italian
Average price: $11-30
Area: Noe Valley
Address: 4109 24th St
San Francisco, CA 94114
Phone: (415) 282-5872

#433
Bender's Bar and Grill
Cuisines: Dive Bar, American
Average price: Under $10
Area: Mission
Address: 806 S Van Ness Ave
San Francisco, CA 94110
Phone: (415) 824-1800

#434
Little Griddle
Cuisines: American, Breakfast & Brunch
Average price: $11-30
Area: Civic Center
Address: 1400 Market St
San Francisco, CA 94102
Phone: (415) 864-4292

#435
Mission Banh Mi Duc Loi Kitchen
Cuisines: Sandwiches, Vietnamese
Average price: Under $10
Area: Mission
Address: 2200 Mission St
San Francisco, CA 94110
Phone: (415) 551-1773

#436
Perbacco
Cuisines: Italian
Average price: $31-60
Area: Financial District
Address: 230 California St
San Francisco, CA 94111
Phone: (415) 955-0663

#437
La Corneta Taqueria
Cuisines: Mexican, Caterer
Average price: Under $10
Area: Glen Park
Address: 2834 Diamond St
San Francisco, CA 94131
Phone: (415) 469-8757

#438
Mymy
Cuisines: Breakfast & Brunch, Burgers
Average price: $11-30
Area: Nob Hill
Address: 1500 California St
San Francisco, CA 94109
Phone: (415) 800-7466

#439
Aperto Restaurant
Cuisines: Italian, Breakfast & Brunch
Average price: $11-30
Area: Potrero Hill
Address: 1434 18th St
San Francisco, CA 94107
Phone: (415) 252-1625

#440
Ambrosia Bakery
Cuisines: Bakery, Sandwiches
Average price: $11-30
Area: Lakeside
Address: 2605 Ocean Ave
San Francisco, CA 94132
Phone: (415) 334-5305

#441
Bullshead Restaurant
Cuisines: Steakhouse, Burgers
Average price: $11-30
Area: West Portal
Address: 840 Ulloa St
San Francisco, CA 94127
Phone: (415) 665-4350

#442
Thai Cottage Restaurant
Cuisines: Thai
Average price: $11-30
Area: Outer Sunset
Address: 4041 Judah St
San Francisco, CA 94122
Phone: (415) 566-5311

#443
Jay'n Bee Club
Cuisines: American, Dive Bar
Average price: Under $10
Area: Mission
Address: 2736 20th St
San Francisco, CA 94110
Phone: (415) 824-4190

#444
Basil Thai Restaurant & Bar
Cuisines: Thai
Average price: $11-30
Area: SoMa
Address: 1175 Folsom St
San Francisco, CA 94103
Phone: (415) 552-8999

#445
Ame
Cuisines: American, Japanese
Average price: Above $61
Area: Financial District, SoMa
Address: 689 Mission St
San Francisco, CA 94105
Phone: (415) 284-4040

#446
Cotogna
Cuisines: Italian
Average price: $31-60
Area: Financial District
Address: 490 Pacific Ave
San Francisco, CA 94133
Phone: (415) 775-8508

#447
House of Thai
Cuisines: Thai
Average price: $11-30
Area: Tenderloin
Address: 901 Larkin St
San Francisco, CA 94109
Phone: (415) 441-2248

#448
Cookie Time
Cuisines: Desserts, Food Stand
Average price: Under $10
Area: Castro
Address: 3859 24th St
San Francisco, CA 94114
Phone: (415) 735-5055

#449
Piccino
Cuisines: Pizza, Sandwiches
Average price: $11-30
Area: Dogpatch, Potrero Hill
Address: 1001 Minnesota St
San Francisco, CA 94107
Phone: (415) 824-4224

#450
Toy Boat Dessert Café
Cuisines: Ice Cream, Coffee & Tea
Average price: Under $10
Area: Inner Richmond
Address: 401 Clement St
San Francisco, CA 94118
Phone: (415) 751-7505

#451
Blackwood
Cuisines: Thai, Breakfast & Brunch, Asian Fusion
Average price: $11-30
Area: Marina/Cow Hollow
Address: 2150 Chestnut St
San Francisco, CA 94123
Phone: (415) 931-9663

#452
Super Duper Burgers
Cuisines: Burgers, American
Average price: Under $10
Area: Financial District, Union Square
Address: 721 Market St
San Francisco, CA 94103
Phone: (415) 538-3437

#453
Mexico Tipico
Cuisines: Mexican
Average price: Under $10
Area: Excelsior, Outer Mission
Address: 4581 Mission St
San Francisco, CA 94112
Phone: (415) 337-7562

#454
Pachino Trattoria & Pizzeria
Cuisines: Pizza, Italian
Average price: $11-30
Area: Financial District
Address: 318 Kearny St
San Francisco, CA 94104
Phone: (415) 956-4056

#455
Manora's Thai Cuisine
Cuisines: Thai
Average price: $11-30
Area: SoMa
Address: 1600 Folsom St
San Francisco, CA 94103
Phone: (415) 861-6224

#456
Caffe Sport
Cuisines: Italian, Seafood
Average price: $11-30
Area: North Beach/Telegraph Hill
Address: 574 Green St
San Francisco, CA 94133
Phone: (415) 981-1251

#457
Tropisueño
Cuisines: Mexican
Average price: $11-30
Area: Financial District, SoMa
Address: 75 Yerba Buena Ln
San Francisco, CA 94103
Phone: (415) 243-0299

#458
Cafe du Soleil
Cuisines: Coffee & Tea, Sandwiches
Average price: Under $10
Area: Hayes Valley, Lower Haight
Address: 200 Fillmore St
San Francisco, CA 94102
Phone: (415) 934-8637

#459
Cafe Zitouna
Cuisines: Moroccan, African
Average price: $11-30
Area: Tenderloin
Address: 1201 Sutter St
San Francisco, CA 94109
Phone: (415) 673-2622

#460
Shufat Market
Cuisines: Deli, Sandwiches
Average price: Under $10
Area: Noe Valley
Address: 3807 24th St
San Francisco, CA 94114
Phone: (415) 826-6207

#461
Buster's
Cuisines: American, Cheesesteaks
Average price: Under $10
Area: North Beach/Telegraph Hill
Address: 366 Columbus Ave
San Francisco, CA 94133
Phone: (415) 392-2800

#462
Mela Tandoori Kitchen
Cuisines: Indian, Pakistani
Average price: $11-30
Area: Civic Center
Address: 536 Golden Gate Ave
San Francisco, CA 94102
Phone: (415) 447-4041

#463
La Traviata
Cuisines: Italian
Average price: $11-30
Area: Mission
Address: 2854 Mission St
San Francisco, CA 94110
Phone: (415) 282-0500

#464
Sodini's Green Valley Restaurant
Cuisines: Italian
Average price: $11-30
Area: North Beach/Telegraph Hill
Address: 510 Green St
San Francisco, CA 94133
Phone: (415) 291-0499

#465
Roxie's Market & Deli
Cuisines: Sandwiches, Grocery
Average price: Under $10
Area: Inner Sunset
Address: 500 Kirkham St
San Francisco, CA 94122
Phone: (415) 731-0982

#466
All Good Pizza
Cuisines: Pizza, Sandwiches, Salad
Average price: $11-30
Area: Bayview-Hunters Point
Address: 1605 Jerrold Ave
San Francisco, CA 94124
Phone: (415) 933-9384

#467
Mario's Bohemian Cigar Store Cafe
Cuisines: Italian, Sandwiches, Bar
Average price: Under $10
Area: North Beach/Telegraph Hill
Address: 566 Columbus Ave
San Francisco, CA 94133
Phone: (415) 362-0536

#468
Cafe Reverie
Cuisines: Coffee & Tea, Sandwiches
Average price: $11-30
Area: Cole Valley
Address: 848 Cole St
San Francisco, CA 94117
Phone: (415) 242-0200

#469
Dosa On Fillmore
Cuisines: Indian
Average price: $31-60
Area: Japantown, Lower Pacific Heights
Address: 1700 Fillmore St
San Francisco, CA 94115
Phone: (415) 441-3672

#470
Lime Tree Southeast Asian Kitchen
Cuisines: Singaporean, Malaysian, Indonesian
Average price: Under $10
Area: Inner Sunset
Address: 450 Irving St
San Francisco, CA 94122
Phone: (415) 665-1415

#471
Coqueta
Cuisines: Spanish, Tapas
Average price: $31-60
Area: Embarcadero
Address: The Embarcadero
San Francisco, CA 94105
Phone: (415) 704-8866

#472
AsiaSF
Cuisines: Asian Fusion
Average price: $31-60
Area: SoMa
Address: 201 9th St
San Francisco, CA 94103
Phone: (415) 255-2742

#473
Due Drop In
Cuisines: Middle Eastern, American
Average price: Under $10
Area: Castro
Address: 489 Church St
San Francisco, CA 94114
Phone: (415) 626-3767

#474
Crepe Temptations
Cuisines: Desserts, Crêpes
Average price: Under $10
Area: Outer Sunset
Address: 2575 Judah St
San Francisco, CA 94122
Phone: (415) 379-4892

#475
Market Mayflower and Deli
Cuisines: Deli, Fruits & Veggies
Average price: $11-30
Area: Nob Hill
Address: 985 Bush St
San Francisco, CA 94109
Phone: (415) 474-6110

#476
Angkor Borei
Cuisines: Cambodian
Average price: $11-30
Area: Bernal Heights, Mission
Address: 3471 Mission St
San Francisco, CA 94110
Phone: (415) 550-8417

#477
In-N-Out Burger
Cuisines: Fast Food, Burgers
Average price: Under $10
Area: Fisherman's Wharf, North Beach/Telegraph Hill
Address: 333 Jefferson St
San Francisco, CA 94133
Phone: (800) 786-1000

#478
theLab - Temp.
Cuisines: Cafe
Average price: $11-30
Area: Dogpatch, Potrero Hill
Address: 801 22nd St
San Francisco, CA 94107
Phone: (415) 489-2881

#479
Blue Danube Coffee House
Cuisines: Coffee & Tea, Cafe
Average price: Under $10
Area: Inner Richmond
Address: 306 Clement St
San Francisco, CA 94118
Phone: (415) 221-9041

#480
Michael Mina
Cuisines: American
Average price: Above $61
Area: Financial District
Address: 252 California St
San Francisco, CA 94111
Phone: (415) 397-9222

#481
Delessio Market & Bakery
Cuisines: Bakery, Deli, Caterer
Average price: $11-30
Area: SoMa
Address: 1695 Market St
San Francisco, CA 94103
Phone: (415) 552-5559

#482
Amawele's South African Kitchen
Cuisines: South African, Specialty Food
Average price: Under $10
Area: Financial District, SoMa
Address: 101 Spear St
San Francisco, CA 94105
Phone: (415) 536-5900

#483
Pomelo
Cuisines: Asian Fusion, Breakfast & Brunch, European
Average price: $11-30
Area: Noe Valley
Address: 1793 Church St
San Francisco, CA 94131
Phone: (415) 285-2257

#484
Nick's Crispy Tacos
Cuisines: Mexican, Lounge
Average price: Under $10
Area: Russian Hill
Address: 1500 Broadway
San Francisco, CA 94109
Phone: (415) 409-8226

#485
Akiko's Restaurant
Cuisines: Sushi Bar, Japanese
Average price: $11-30
Area: Chinatown, Financial District
Address: 431 Bush St
San Francisco, CA 94108
Phone: (415) 397-3218

#486
Zarzuela
Cuisines: Spanish, Tapas Bar, Basque
Average price: $11-30
Area: Russian Hill
Address: 2000 Hyde St
San Francisco, CA 94109
Phone: (415) 346-0800

#487
Yu Zen
Cuisines: Japanese, Sushi Bar
Average price: $11-30
Area: Outer Richmond
Address: 4036 Balboa St
San Francisco, CA 94121
Phone: (415) 386-9800

#488
Zaytoon Mediterranean Wraps
Cuisines: Mediterranean, Sandwiches
Average price: Under $10
Area: Mission
Address: 1136 Valencia St
San Francisco, CA 94110
Phone: (415) 824-1787

#489
Vicoletto
Cuisines: Italian
Average price: $11-30
Area: North Beach/Telegraph Hill
Address: 550 Green St
San Francisco, CA 94133
Phone: (415) 433-5800

#490
All Star Donuts
Cuisines: Donuts, Sandwiches
Average price: Under $10
Area: Inner Richmond
Address: 901 Clement St
San Francisco, CA 94118
Phone: (415) 221-9838

#491
Tin Vietnamese Cuisine
Cuisines: Vietnamese
Average price: $11-30
Area: SoMa
Address: 937 Howard St
San Francisco, CA 94103
Phone: (415) 882-7188

#492
Tempest
Cuisines: American
Average price: Under $10
Area: SoMa
Address: 431 Natoma St
San Francisco, CA 94103
Phone: (415) 495-1863

#493
Market & Rye
Cuisines: Sandwiches, American, Breakfast & Brunch
Average price: $11-30
Area: Potrero Hill
Address: 300 De Haro St
San Francisco, CA 94103
Phone: (415) 252-7455

#494
Marnee Thai
Cuisines: Thai
Average price: $11-30
Area: Outer Sunset
Address: 2225 Irving St
San Francisco, CA 94122
Phone: (415) 665-9500

#495
Pancho Villa Taqueria
Cuisines: Mexican
Average price: Under $10
Area: Mission
Address: 3071 16th St
San Francisco, CA 94103
Phone: (415) 864-8840

#496
MunchBoxx
Cuisines: Vietnamese, Sandwiches
Average price: Under $10
Area: Financial District
Address: 643 Clay St
San Francisco, CA 94111
Phone: (415) 277-7208

#497
Saffron Grill
Cuisines: Indian
Average price: $11-30
Area: Alamo Square
Address: 1279 Fulton St
San Francisco, CA 94117
Phone: (415) 567-5100

#498
Yukol Place Thai Cuisine
Cuisines: Thai
Average price: $11-30
Area: Marina/Cow Hollow
Address: 2380 Lombard St
San Francisco, CA 94123
Phone: (415) 922-1599

#499
Mescolanza
Cuisines: Italian
Average price: $11-30
Area: Outer Richmond
Address: 2221 Clement St
San Francisco, CA 94121
Phone: (415) 668-2221

#500
Izakaya Sozai
Cuisines: Japanese, Tapas
Average price: $11-30
Area: Inner Sunset
Address: 1500 Irving St
San Francisco, CA 94122
Phone: (415) 742-5122

Made in United States
Cleveland, OH
08 June 2025